THE INSTITUTION OF SATI IN INDIA

THE INSTITUTION OF SATI IN INDIA

REENA MISHRA

ABHIJEET PUBLICATIONS
DELHI 110094

ABHIJEET PUBLICATIONS
2/46 Tukhmeerpur Extension
Delhi-110 094
Phone: 011-22960492, 65698474
E-mail: abhijeetpublication@gmail.com

THE INSTITUTION OF SATI IN INDIA

First Published 2009

ISBN 978-81-89886-93-6

PRINTED IN INDIA

Published by J.K. Singh for Abhijeet Publications, Delhi-110 094, Lasertypeset by Gaurav Graphics, New Delhi and Printed at Himanshu Printers, Delhi.

Dedicated to the
Sacred Memory of my Mother,
SMT. SAVITRI JHA
as a token of respect and gratitude.

Preface

Sati is a funeral practice among some Hindu communities in which a recently-widowed woman would immolate herself on her husband's funeral pyre.

The term is derived from the original name of the goddess Sati also known as Dakshayani, who immolated herself, unable to bear her father Daksha's humiliation of her (living) husband Shiva. The term may also be used to refer to the widow herself. The term sati is now sometimes interpreted as 'chaste woman'. With strict laws against Sati, the practice has now become rare.

The ritual has prehistoric roots, and many parallels from other cultures are known. Many ancient cultures in Mediterranean, Central Asian and even Chinese regions had a similar practice.

Aristobulus of Cassandreia, a Greek historian, who travelled to India with the expedition of Alexander of Macedon, recorded the practice of sati at the city of Taxila. A later instance of voluntary co-cremation appears in an account of an Indian soldier in the army of Eumenes of Cardia, whose two wives vied to die on his funeral pyre, in 316 BC. The Greeks believed that the practice had been instituted to discourage wives from poisoning their husbands.

Voluntary death at funerals has been described in northern India before the Gupta empire. The original practices were called *anumarana*, and were uncommon. *Anumarana* was not comparable to later understandings of sati, since the practices were not restricted to widows — rather, anyone, male or female, with personal loyalty to the deceased could commit suicide at a loved one's funeral. These included the deceased's relatives, servants, followers, or friends. Sometimes these deaths stemmed from vows of loyalty. *Sahamarana,* was the generally accepted and widely practiced form of Sati, in which the widows used to burn themselves alongwith the dead body of their husbands.

Widow burning, the practice as understood today, started to become more extensive after the end of the Gupta empire, around A.D. 500 . The rise of the practice has been variously ascribed to the decline of Buddhism in India, the rise of caste-based societies, and introduction by the Huna invaders who contributed to the fall of the Gupta empire. It has also been attributed to the Muslim conquest of India.

At about this time, instances of sati began to be marked by inscribed memorial stones. The earliest of these are found in Sagar, Madhya Pradesh, though the largest collections date from several centuries later, and are found in Rajasthan. These stones, called *devli,* or sati-stones, became shrines to the dead woman, who was treated as an object of reverence and worship. They are most common in western India.

By about the 10th century sati, as understood today, was known across much of the subcontinent. It continued to occur, usually at a low frequency and with regional variations, until the early 19th century.

Attempts to limit or ban the practice had been made by individual British officers in the 18th century, but without the backing of the British East India Company. The first formal British ban was imposed in 1798, in the city of Calcutta only. The practice continued in surrounding regions. Toward the end of the 18th century, the evangelical church in Britain, and its members in India, started campaigns against sati. Leaders of these included William

Carey and William Wilberforce, and both appeared to be motivated partly by a desire to convert Indians to Christianity. These movements put pressure on the Company to ban the act, and the Bengal Presidency started collecting figures on the practice in 1813.

From about 1812, the Raja Rammohan Roy started his own campaign against the practice. He was motivated by the experience of seeing his own sister-in-law commit sati. Among his actions, he visited Calcutta cremation grounds to persuade widows not to so die, formed watch groups to do the same, and wrote and disseminated articles to show that it was not required by scripture.

On 4 December 1829, the practice was formally banned in the Bengal Presidency lands, by the then governor, Lord William Bentinck. The ban was challenged in the courts, and the matter went to the Privy Council in London, but was upheld in 1832. Other company territories also banned it shortly after. Although the original ban in Bengal was fairly uncompromising, later in the century British laws include provisions that provided mitigation for murder when "the person whose death is caused, being above the age of 18 years, suffers death or takes the risk of death with his own consent".

Sati remained legal in some princely states for a time after it had been abolished in lands under British control. The last such state to permit it, Jaipur, banned the practice in 1846. Even after that till today there occur reports of sati in newspapers sporadically.

The book tries to make an indepth study of the institution of sati, dealing with topics like Origin of Sati Custom, The Scriptural Sanction of the Sati Pratha, Sati in Literature, Sati in Inscriptions, Foreign Accounts of Sati, Protests Against Sati, Regulation and Prohibition of Sati, Sati After Bentinck, Causes of Sati, and the feminist explanation of Sati.

REENA MISHRA

Acknowledgements

I am indebted to a large number of individuals and institutions who provided help, guidance and co-operation in the preparation of this study. I am grateful to late Prof. (Dr.) Upendra Thakur, former Professor and Head, Department of Ancient Indian and Asian Studies, Magadh University, Bodh Gaya, who encouraged me to study this problem. I am indebted to Dr. S.N. Sahay, Professor & Head, Department of Ancient Indian and Asian Studies, Magadh University, Bodh-Gaya, who despite his busy schedule and indifferent health, supervised my work. I am thankful to Dr. Md. Aquique, Professor, Department of Ancient Indian & Asian Studies, and other teachers of the department for their encouragement and help. I am also grateful to my father—Dr. Dayadhar Jha, Professor of Political Science, Magadh University, Bodh-Gaya, who helped me to locate the references. I am also thankful to the members of my family—my father-in-law, Shri Gopalji Mishra, my brother-in-law, Shri Shantan Jib Mishra and Anant Jib Mishra, who encouraged me in my work. I am indebted to my husband—Dr. Chiranjib Mishra for encouragement and help. I express my thanks to my mother— Smt. Savitri Devi, my brothers Shankar and Santosh and sister Meena, who took care of my son Shailesh while I was busy in this study. I am really thankful to my younger son Monu who was deprived of my love and care while I was busy in writing this work.

I would like to put on record my thanks to Dr. S.N. Mishra, Professor of Rural Studies, Indian Institute of Public Administration, New Delhi, who helped me in getting this book published.

I thank the authorities of Magadh University who awarded me a scholarship to complete the study.

I am thankful to Dr. Naval Kishore Upadhyay, who typed my work. For any defect in the study, however, I am alone responsible.

Last but not the least I am thankful to Shri Jitendra Singh, M/s. Abhijeet Publications, Delhi, for bringing out the book in a nice form and that too within short time.

REENA MISHRA

Contents

1

Introduction

Sati is a feminine noun formed from the verbal root *Sat,* meaning what is real, true, good, or virtuous. A *Sati,* therefore, signified a woman whom her religion considered as good and virtuous if she sought death on the decease of her husband and was burned along with his corpse.[1] The root meaning of the word is essential being. But she who refuses to live when her husband is dead is called *Sati* in a more special sense.[2]

Thus the word Sati, meaning a virtuous wife, applies to a practice once prevalent in India among the higher castes of Brahmins and Rajputs. On the death of her husband a Brahmin or high caste widow would proclaim herself Sati, and at the cremation throw herself over her husband's body on the funeral pyre, having first distributed her jewels among the assembled mourners.[3] Since the self-immolation of a widow on her husband's funeral pyre came to be regarded in India as the supreme demonstration of wifely devotion, early British officials and missionaries used the word Sati (Suttee) to designate the practice itself as well as the devoted wife.[4]

Thus there prevailed in India customary rite involving the "concremation of the living wife with the dead husband".[5] Sometimes it involved co-internment, and rarely co-immersion.[6] To this rite was applied the name of Suttee in 1787 for the first time with any measure of exactness.[7]

Thus by this term is meant the rite whereby the widow burnt herself at the funeral pyre of her husband. Sometimes, especially with kings, officers, servants, and horses etc. Were also cremated along with wives. The term Satin however refers only to the concremation of wives and concubines. In the last legal case of Sati in Udaipur in 1861, when all the legal wives of the Maharaja refused, "a slave girl was induced to become a Sati."[8] The form Sati is also used as a variant and both the forms mean both the rite of widow immolation and the widow so immolated. When the former sense is to be distinguished from the later, the widow is described as having committed Sati or become one. Edward Thomson tried to distinguish between the two usages by using Sati for the person and Suttee for the rite.[9] But the attempt did not succeed. Most dictionaries use the two forms interchangeably.

Some authorities feel that etymological connection between the Sanskrit term Sati, which means chaste wife and which is also the name of a Hindu goddess, and the practice of widow-self-immolation is erroneous.[10] It has been remarked[11] that "the Sanskrit word *Sati* is a feminine noun meaning "good", "devout", "true" and consequently it denotes a person and not a practice. The application of the substantive to the act instead of to the person is European."

However, Arvind Sharma[12] suggests that the form to commit Sati or to become sati has an Indian parallel. A popular Hindi couplet takes a fling at womanly wantonness thus:

Tiriya Charit jane na Koi,

Pati mar Ke Satti hoi.

This may be paraphrase as female character is inscrutable. She is capable of "becoming a Sati" after killing her own husband.[13] Sharma says that he "has not been able to date the saying; if it is Pre-18th Century, then the expression "becoming Suttee" would seem to have roots in Indian use; if not, this might be a feedback into Hindi of the English usage".[14]

Sati, in Hindu usage, was known as *sahamaran* when the widow underwent immolation along with her dead husband and *anumaran* when the immolation occurred after the husband's cremation. The expressions *Sahagaman* and *Anugaman* were also sometimes used.

In Hindu usage Sati also refers to a goddess, the wife of Shiva who immolated herself to avenge her husband's insult at the hands of her father.

The present study confines itself to the practice of widow immolation.

Burning of widows was common enough among many ancient tribes and primitive religious communities. Schrader[15] states that Indo-Germanic custom ordained that the wife should die with her husband, and this custom he ascribes to the desire to provide the deceased with what was dear to him during life as well as "to make the life of the house-father safe on all sides, and to render him an object of perpetual care and anxiety to his family."

Ancient Greek, German, Slav, Chinese and other civilizations also had similar customs and Kings and nobles were put in their graves with their arms, slaves, servants and ministers.[16] J. Talboys Wheeler[17] writes that "the slaughter of a wife or concubine at the obsequies of a deceased husband seems to have ben a Scythian custom. It was an outgrowth of a belief in ghosts. The dead man was supposed to require the society of a favourite wife or concubine in the world of shades".

It is somewhat remarkable that in the ancient Vedic rite of cremation there is no authentic appearance of Sati, or the sacrifice of the living wife or concubine in the burning place of the dead man, in order that the female might accompany his spirit to the world of shades. It would, therefore, appear that the propitiation of ghosts led to no such horrible sacrifices among the Vedic Aryans. The mourners offered cakes and water in the simple belief that the spirits of departed heroes were conscious of such pious attentions; and to this day such a faith still lingers in the affections to soften and humanize the world. The Aryans appear to have had no such custom. The *Atharvaved,* however, refers to a very ancient custom of widow burning which was given up by the Aryans. After the great battle between the Pandavas and Kaurvas, the dead bodies of the slain were burnt on funeral pyres, but none of the widows were burnt with them . None of the queens of Dasaratha were put to death at his funeral obsequies. If a man died childless, his widow was expected to bear a son the nearest kinsman but otherwise the widows of a king continued to live in the royal palace under the protection of his successor.

The original distinction between the Scythian and Aryan usage is thus obvious. The Scythians slaughtered a living female to enable her to accompany the dead man, the Aryans placed the widows in charge of the new head of the family. Both usages found expression among the Rajupts. The dead man was burnt according to the Aryan fashion; but the living widow was burnt with him in order that she might accompany her husband to the world of spirits.

The rite of Sati, as practised by the Rajputs, may thus be described as a Scythian usage modified by Aryan culture. The bodies, dead and living, were no longer buried, but burnt. The female was no longer slaughtered as an unwilling victim to the selfish sensuality of a barbarian on the contrary, she was the widow of a high-soulded Rajput; the reflex of his chivalrous devotion; prepared to perish with him in order that she might accompany her deceased Lord to a heaven of felicity. The Scythian Sati was further modified by the Aryan worship of fire and the Sun. Fire was the purifying deity. She was not only the domestic goddess of the household, but the divine messenger that carried the sacrifice to the gods, the purifying flame that bore away the widow and her Lord to the manions of the Sun. In this manner the horrible rite, so revolting to civilization and humanity, was imbued with an element of the religion of the affections. It elevated the helpless concubine into a self-sacrificing heroine; the distracted widow into a joyful and triumphant bride. The future of the bereaved woman was no longer a vista of shame and sorrow. She ascended the pyre as the chariot of fire which was to carry her away to the arms of her glorified bridegroom in the realms of bliss.

Such was the rite which the Rajputs and the Brahmins carried to nearly every quarter of India and even to those countries where they settled, for example, in countries of South-East Asia. It was considered to be the expression of the highest conjugal affection combined with the lowest state of female degradation. The unfortunate widow had no way of escape from a joyless life of servitude, exception by the most horrible sacrifices. The honour of the family depended on the heroism of the woman; and the widow was too often condemned to the pain of martyrdom when the heroism was altogether wanting. The victim was stupefied with drugs, and adorned as a burnt offering. She was led by the Brahmins and her relatives to the pyre form which flight was impossible. The timber was set on fire by the nearest kinsman and often by her own son, amidst the deafening noise of drums and the cries of an exuviated throng.

The earliest historical reference to this practice comes from Greek historians who came to India during the invasion of Alexander, the Great. The earliest scriptural sanction comes from the *Vishudharma Sutra* written in the early centuries of the Christian era. The first epigraphic record comes from the Gupta period in 510 A.D. The first literary evidence comes from the sacrifice. It is not accidental that matriarchal societies do not observe Sati or enforced widowhood.

Between the end of the Vedic period and 12th Century A.D., the idea seemed to have gained ground that the husband should have exclusive and total control over his wife's sexuality. Pre-pubertal marriage also transferred the responsibility for safeguarding the girl's sexuality form their male kin in her natal family to her husband and his agnates.

Once married, total faith-fulness was expected of the wife, and this was attempted to be assured by the deification of the husband. Total control over her sexuality was not only for the duration of the marriage: it extended to the pre and post-marital periods, absurd a sit may seem to outsiders. Virginity in brides was ensured by pre-pubertal, and frequently, child-marriages, while celibacy was required of the widow. She was disfigured by having her head shaved, and by forbidding to her the symbols of the happy and auspicious state of sumanglihood (i.e. the married state with the husband alive), and her activities were restricted to the kitchen and to ritual. She was condemned to perpetual mourning, as it were and she became a symbol of inauspiciousness and ill-luck. The death of her husband was attributed to the sins she had committed in a previous incarnation. The widow who decided to commit Sati was, on the contrary, the mirror image of the widow who had decided to live.

She was auspicious, and she was dressed as a bride for her last journey. Her martyrdom brought good reputation and good luck to her kinsfolk and to her village.[19]

But in searching for origins it might be as well to consider other situations that prevailed in India. The notion of bride-price, for example, can suggestion some situations the purchase of a woman, the logical termination of which may have been the requirement of her dying with her husband, although this is not typical of bride-price. But perhaps a more acceptable explanation may relate to societies changing their systems of kinship and inheritance. In some circumstances the wife would be as alien in ethereal stages of change. Control over female sexuality would be a further reason. The practice may have originated amount societies in flux and become customary among those holding property such as the families of chiefs and Kshatriyas. Once it was established as a custom associated with the Kshatriyas it would continue to be so among those claiming Kshatriya status as well.[20]

Yet another factor was the woman's role in economic

production. In the families of labouring castes women were an integral part of the productive process and hence of great value in the household economy. In contrast in upper caste/ class families they were economically tied to the 'master' as an object of pleasure. The death of husbands, therefore, rendered their lives irrelevant and, more often than not, they were looked upon as an unnecessary and avoidable burden. If they also inherited the property of their husbands, as in the Dayabhaga system in Bengal, the families stood to gain if the widows were induced to observe the religious rite of Sati.

From the seventeenth to early nineteenth centuries in Bengal a large number of cases of Sati was reported. The overwhelming incidence was among the brahmins of this area. The major cause for this unprecedented rise in widow immolation, particularly in the early nineteenth century has been attributed to the legal system relating to inheritance. By asking Sanskrit Pandits about the laws of property and inheritance, forced burning of many young widows in Bengal, for Manu had prescribed that a childless widow must have a right to property of her husband, which the Dayabhaga text reiterated. However, as there was a gap between actual practice and the view expressed in the texts, the issue did not create any problem. But the rulers' insistence on texts and reliance on Sanskrit Pandits created a situation where young childless widows were encouraged through religious indoctrination to commit Sati, or sometimes subjected to forced burning by greedy for their's or relatives of the deceased. Thus Sati became a means of removing one among the claimants to inheritance.

It is interesting that during the second millennium A.D. when brahmin widows were permitted to become satis, this was also the time when brahmin property holders increased both in numbers as well as in the size of their holdings owing to the land grants which they received from royalty. Thus what was in origin a custom associated with Kshatriya notion of heroism and honour was now converted into a convenient way of eliminating an inheritor. It has been suggested that the largest occurrence was among Kulin brahmin families for the ratio of male to female seems to have been severely out of balance, requiring that the Kulin marry many wives from several families. The effect of this on the ritual of widow immolation was self-evident.[21]

Thus a number of causes have been suggested for the prevalence of this practice.

Though the practice was in vogue in the Punjab, Rajputana, Kashmir, Bengal, Karnataka and Maharashtra and it continued for over two thousand years, voices of protest were raised against this inhuman practice. Thus Bana in his *Kadambari* strongly opposed it. Medhatithi on his commentary on *Manusmriti* considers it as irreligious and against the scriptures. The Tantrikas also condemned this practice. The Sikh Guru Amardas, Chaitanya, Swami Narayan and Raja Ram Mohun Roy opposed this practice strongly.

Still the practice continued and references to its prevalence can be had from literature, inscriptions and foreign accounts. The Muslim rulers of Delhi Sultanate and Mughal emperors tried to regulate this practice. Permission was required before its performance and a classification was made between legal and illegal satis. The Government of Lord Bentinck abolished it in the early part of the nineteenth Century. Still it is performed off and on in Utter Pradesh and Rajasthan.

There is an ambivalent attitude about this practice. Some people consider it as religious suicide, voluntary and, therefore, in conformity with our traditions. Others condemn it as inhuman, oppression of women and against all norms of civilisation.

It is, therefore, necessary to have a comprehensive history of this practice to understand the roots and historical, economic and sociological factors which permitted this inhuman practice. Understanding the history of Sati, its social roots and its ideological underpinnings, therefore, has some pragmatic value today.

The present study is an attempt in this direction. The study has been divided into a number of chapters for the sake of convenience. The first chapter (Introduction) raises the problem and emphasizes importance of the study. Even after a legal ban the forces are at work to support this practice. It is necessary to identify these forces. The second chapter traces the origin of the practice in India. The third chapter discusses the scriptural sanctions behind the practice. Here the Vedic literature, Dharma Sutras and Grihya Sutras have been examined. The Smriti literature seems to sanction it. The fourth chapter discusses the evidence of literature. From the *Mahabharat, Harshacharit, Kadambari, Ratnavali, Priyadarshika, Naganand, Mrichhakatika, Kumarsambhava, Venisamhar* to the poetry of Rabindra Nath Tagore we have ample evidence of this practice. A Semi-historical work, *Rajatarangini* of Kalhana is full of sati references. The Puranas also mention this. The fifth chapter traces the practice on epigraphic sources. A large number of inscriptions are available in various parts of India and Nepal in this connection. Innumerable sati-stones and temples have been erected in honour of the satis. The sixth chapter discusses the foreign accounts left by travellers and missionaries. Arab, African, Portuguese, French, British, Venetian travellers have written quite a lot on this practice. The earliest of them, the Greeks, had first mentioned this practice. In their accounts we find appreciation, condemnation and the possible reasons for this practice.

The Seventh Chapter traces the history of protest against Sati. Right from Bana, Medhatithi, Tantrikas, Sikh Guru Amardas, social reformers and intellectuals condemned this practice. Christian missionaries raised their strong voice against this inhuman practice. Enlightened rulers also tried to regulate it. This chapter discusses these voices of protest.

Chapter eight traces the history of regulation and prohibition of this practice. The Sultans of Delhi, Mughal kings, Portuguese, British and Indian rulers tried to regulate and ban this practice. They had limited success. This chapter discusses the attempts to regulate and prohibit this practice.

The Ninth chapter discusses the prevalence of Sati practice even after its legal prohibition. What are the factors that support this practice, even after its prohibition. Some sociological insight is called for this analysis. An attempt has been made in this direction.

The tenth chapter analyses the cause of Sati. The primitive habit of many tribes, religious merit, sense of honour, economic consideration, sanskritization and many other factors may be mentioned in this connection. An attempt has been made in this chapter to find out the reasons behind this inhuman practice. If Sati is to be properly understood it would require a tracking down of information on widow-burning involving a number of sources pertaining to a range of social groups and with reference to various regions at different points in time. Only when we examine the juxtaposition of kinship, property relations, rights of inheritance, the approach to sexuality, the ethic of hero, attitudes deity and adjustments to social change in the context of our history, will we begin perhaps to understand why and how women were encouraged or forced to become Satis.

The last chapter sums up the study.

It is hoped that the present study, with all its limitations, will unravel some of the factors behind this complex phenomenon. It cannot claim to be last word on the problem but it is hoped that more competent scholars will try their hands and throw light on the topic. This study is an humble attempt on the part of a single student of history.

REFERENCES

1. James Hustings (ed.) *Encyclopaedia of Religion and Ethics*, Vol. XI (Edinburg: T & T Clark, 1958), p. 207.
2. Ananda K. Coomaraswamy, *The Dance of Shiva* (New Delhi: Sagar Publications, 1971), p. 111.
3. D.A. Girling (ed.), *Everyman's Encyclopaedia*, Vol. XI (London: J.M. Dent & Sons Ltd., 1978), p. 468.

4. *Encyclopaedia Americana*, Vol. XXVI (New York: Americana Corporation, 1974), p. 80.
5. Monier Williams, *Indian Wisdom* (London: H. Allen & Co., 1875), p. 258, f.n.2.
6. Edward Thompson, *Suttee* (London: George Allen & Unwin, 1928), p. 39.
7. William Crooke (ed.) *Sir H. Yule and A.C. Burnell's Hobson-Jobson* (Delhi: Munshiram Manoharlal, 1968), p. 878.
8. A.S. Altekar, *The Position of Women in Hindu Civilization* (Delhi: Motilal Banarasidas, 1962), p. 142.
9. Edward Thompson, *Suttee*, op. cit., pp. 15-16.
10. N.M. Penzer, ed., *The Ocean of Story*, Vol. IV (London: Chas. J. Sawyer, 1925), p. 258;

    Edward Thompson, op. cit., p. 15.
11. *Encyclopaedia Britannica*, Vol. XXI (London: William Benton, 1969), p. 466.
12. Arvind Sharma, *Sati* (Delhi: Motilal Banarsidass, 1988), p. 86, fn. 9.
13. The idea conveyed by this couplet is beautifully expressed by Kalhan when he writes:

    दौ:शील्यमप्याचरनत्यो द्यातयनौ ऽपि वल्लभान।

    हेलया प्रविशन्त्यग्निं नस्त्रोषु प्रत्ययः कूर्वावत्।।
14. Arvind Sharma, *op. cit.*, p. 86.
15. Schrader, *Pre-historic Antiquities of the Aryan Peoples*, (London: 1890), p. 391.
16. Westermarck, *Origin and Development of Moral Ideas*, Vol. I, 1906, pp. 472-76.
17. J. Talboys Wheeler, *India From the Earliest Ages* (Delhi: Cosmo Publications, 1973), p. 89.
18. K.N. Panikkar, Review of *Sati:* a historical, Social and Philosophical enquiry into the Hindu rite of widow burning by V.N. Dutta in *Seminar* Feb. 1988, p. 45.
19. M.N. Srinivas, Foreword to Arvind Sharma, *Sati, op. cit.*, pp. XII-XIII.
20. Romila Thapar, "In History," *Seminar*, Feb. 88, p. 15.
21. *Ibid.*, p. 18.

2

Origin of the Sati Custom

In prehistoric times there prevailed a belief in several societies that the life and deeds of the dead in the next world are more or less similar to those in this life. It, therefore, became a pious duty of surviving relations to provide a dead person with all the things that he usually needed when alive. Especially when an important personage like a king, a nobleman or a warrior died, it was felt that his usual paraphernalia should be 'sent' with him. He would, of course, require his wives, horses and servants in the next world, and it would, therefore, be necessary and desirable to kill these all, and burn or bury them with him. Such a belief should have given rise to the custom of burning or burying the husband also along with the wife. Man, however, wielded supreme power in society almost everywhere and was not prepared to sanction a custom adverse to this own interest and comfort. It may, however, be pointed out that in Ashanti, King's sisters were allowed to marry handsome youths among commoners, but they were compelled to commit suicide on the death of their royal consorts.[1]

The custom "owes its origin to the oldest religious views and superstitious practice of mankind in general."[2] This practice was widely prevalent amount the ancient Greeks, Germans, Slaves, Egyptians and other races of the world.[3] But a close scrutiny of the available data demonstrates that this was generally confined to the greatones-the princes and the nobbles. When the ancient Scythians buried a King, they strangled one of his concubines, and buried her with him, together with his cup-bearer, cook, groom, waiting-man, messenger and favourite horses.[4] Amongst the Thracians there existed a still more significant custom. Every Thracians there had several wives, and whenever a man died, a sharp contest ensued among his wives as to which of them he loved the most. On such an occasion a number of men and women assembled to hear the dispute, and finally settle the question, and when the most beloved woman had been chosen, she received the praises of all present, and was then slain over the grave by her next of kin, and buried with her husband, whilst all the others are said to have been sorely grieved at not being thought worthy to follow their husband.[5] from Greece we have the instances of Evadne throwing herself in the funeral pyre of her husband and of the suicide of three Messenian widows mentioned by Pausanias. Sacrifice of widows occurred, as it seems a regular custom, among the Scandinavians, Heruli and Slavians".[6] Ralston remarks that "the fact that, in Slovonic lands, a thousand years ago widows used to destroy themselves in order to accompany their dead husbands to the world of spirits, seems to rest on incontestable evidence" and "if the dead was a man of means and distinction he was solaced by the sacrifice of his slaves".[7] Further, "funeral offerings of slaves occurred among the Tentors and the Gauls of Ceasar's time, and in the *Illiad* (of Homer) we read of twelve captives being laid on the funeral pyre of Petroclus."

The custom of the sacrifice of the widow at the funeral of her husband was widely prevalent in ancient times. There is no direct evidence to show that it prevailed in the Indo-European age, but the fact that it was practised among the Gauls, the Goths, the Norwegians, the Celts, the Staves the Thracians would justify the inference that it was probably well established among the Indo-Europeans. It was quite common among the Scythians.[8]

In China if a widow killed herself in order to follow her husband to heaven, her corpse was taken out in a great procession. The system was deep-rooted in China, and in spite of imperial prohibitions, sutteeism of widowed wives and brides continued to flourish in China down to the present Century and met with the same public applause as ever; whilst those widowed wives and brides who lost their lives in preserving their chastity, are entitled both to an honorary gate and to a place in a temple of the state as an object of worship.[9]

In Ancient Egypt there was a practice of forced self-immolation. W.M. Flinders Petrie observes that "in the first dynasty it was the custom to kill off the court and high officials, over five hundred first at the king's death; the custom dwindled to about a tenth by the end of the dynasty."[10] There are various references to human sacrifices in the *Book of The dead*. Plutarch, quoting from Manetho, states that at El Kab they used to burn men alive, giving the name of *set* (name of god of Evil in Egypt). Women's adultery was punished by forcing them to burn themselves before the harem. In Japan and China, the original immolations were replaced by the custom of allowing the nearest relatives and slaves of the deceased simply to settle on the tomb, instead of interring in there to sacrifice to the manes, and by prohibiting widows from remarrying."

The general prevalence of this custom among the primitive warlike tribes is not difficult to understand. Fighting races are very jealous of their women and after prefer to kill the, rather than take the risk of their astray after their husbands death. There was also the general belief, already referred to, that the warrior would require in his next life all those things that were near and dear to him in this existence. It was, therefore, as reasonable to bury his clothes, bow, arrows and horses as to inter his wife. The wife is usually the dearest relation of a man, and the visitations of a chief's ghost were popularly attributed to his desire to be united with his quondam queen. Why not lessen these dreaded visitations by burning or burying her along with his remains? This custom also made the life of the patriarch very safe; it practically eliminated all possibility of any one among his numerous mutually envious wives intriguing against his life. They all knew that even if successful, they had no chance of surviving him. They were, therefore, all care and attention to see that no preventible accident intervened to shorten the husband's life.[12] According to D.D. Kosambi:

> The origin of the much discussed *sati* immolation of the widow with her husband's corpse now seems fairly obvious. The first widow in Greek myth to survive her husband and remarry rather than enter his flaming pyre was Gorgophone, daughter of Prerseus. Widow-burning can only have developed from suppression of matriarchal tradition, presumably as a warning or precaution against its surreptitious revival. We must remember that the ordinary tribesman knew only group-marriage in both types of society, not the chief's hierosgamos. So 'husband' some chieftain or sacred King who gained his title to sovereignty (over the new society fused out of two distinct types) primarily by formal marriage to some local high-priestess or 'queen'. If, then, the husband died, there were ample grounds for suspicion that it was the wife's doing, a reversion to the old ritual. The *Sati* custom would not only discourage this, but act like a curious inversion of the older sacrifice; and count further as provision for the departed leader in the next world. Yet, the *Sati* is herself not on the same level as the dead hero's horse, bow, panoply and accoutrements immolated with him for she immediately becomes a goddess, with her own cult. The ancient but still recited marriage hymn (RV. X. 85. 44 admonishes the bride *a-pati-ghnee edhi* —become a non-husband killer. This excellent advice is followed up with an invocation to Indra to give her ten sons and to make her husband the eleventh. This would carry the proper meaning only in a society which had not completely forgotten that the husband was once sent to the gods in sacrifice, but never the son".[13] So far as India is concerned, a similar practice prevailed in the frontier areas. "The beauty, loving nature, and the utter fidelity of the Madra and Bahlika women remained

> proverbial. A warrior's widow in those regions would even immolate herself with her husband's corpse. This horrifying custom of sati was then completely unknown in the east and would so remain till early feudal times, say the sixth Century A.D."[14]

From the Lothal (one of the important sites of Indus Valley Civilization) cemetery comes evidence of the burial of pairs of skeletons, one male and one female in each case, interred in a single grave. It has been suggested that these may indicate a practice akin to Sati.[15]

We have seen that the custom of sacrificing the wife at the husband's death existed among the Aryans in the Indo-European period. By the time they entered India, it had, however, gone out of vogue. E do not find it mentioned in the *Vesta*. Nor is it referred to in the funeral hymns of the *Rigveda*, where it would certainly have been mentioned if it had been in existence.

The *Atharvaveda*, however, shows that the funeral ritual of the Vedic age preserved some formalities reminiscent of the archaic custom of Sati. It shows that it was still customary for the widow to lie by the side of her husband's corpse on the funeral pyre; she was, however, asked to come down, and a prayer was offered that she should lead a prosperous life enjoying the bliss of children and wealth.[16] It is, therefore, clear that the Vedic age expected the widow rather to remarry than to immolate herself.

The reasons that led to the discontinuation of the Sati custom in the vedic age can only be inferred. Probably the finer cultural outlook, that the vedic Aryans had developed by this time, had convinced them that the custom was a barbarous one. Probably they found themselves in minority in India and felt the compelling necessity to increase their population in order to ensure their political domination. Instead of allowing widows to be burnt, they thought that it would be better to encourage them to live and increase the population by levirate or remarriage.[17] On the whole the position of women was fairly satisfactory in the vedic age. Girls were educated like boys and had to pass through a period of Brahmacharya. Some of them became distinguished poetesses, and the poems of some of them have been honoured by their inclusion in the canonical literature. The marriage of girls used to take place at a fairly advanced age of 17-18 Educated brides of this age had some effective voice in the selection of their partners in life. Very often there were love marriages, which were later blessed by parents. There was no seclusion of women; they used to move freely in society, often even in the company of their lovers. In social and religious gatherings they occupied a prominent position. They had an absolute equality with men in the eye of religion; they could perform sacrifices independently. Marriage, in fact, was a religious necessity to both the man and the woman, neither could reach heaven without being accompanied by his duly married consort. The position of the wife was an honoured one in the family.[18]

The relatively more satisfactory position of women in the vedic age was due to political and religious reasons. As a rule in a community, which is civilised and is moving in search of pastures fresh and new, women occupy an honourable position. Men are mostly engrossed in military or semi-military activities, and they have to rely to a very great extent on the help and co-operation of women in the normal spheres and activities of family life. Their womenfolk help them in agricultural activities as well as in animal husbandry. Under such circumstances women can clearly and convincingly demonstrate to men that they are most parasites, but very useful members of society, whose cooperation is very valuable in securing prosperity in peace and victory in war.

It would appear that the general freedom and better status which women enjoyed in the vedic age were largely due to men being engrossed in the work of conquest and consolidation. Women used to take an active part in agriculture, animal husbandry and manufacture of cloth, bows, arrows and other war material. They were thus useful members of society, and could not be, therefore, treated with an air of patronage or contempt. The cheap or forced labour to the enslaved population was not yet available to the Aryans for tasks mentioned above.[19]

It may be pointed out that women in the age of Homer (1000 B.C.) occupied a much more honourable position in Greek society than they did in the days of Pericles (500 B.C.). Causes were more or less similar. In the Homeric age women were productive and valuable members of society. They worked as hard as men, and managed the household without much cooperation from their male relations or slaves. The whole process of garment-marketing was under their supervision in Greece, as it was in India. They brought water, they washed clothes, they tended chattels, they cooked food. In the age of Pericles slavery had become an established institution and all manual work in the household was done by slaves. The wife lost nearly all her occupations. She became a parasite and society ceased to respect her.

The exigencies of the political situation in the Vedic period were responsible for the abolition of the prehistoric Sati custom and sanctioning of Niyoga and remarriage. Like Hitler and Mussolini, Vedic chiefs were anixous for heroes, more heroes, and still more heroes. The gospel they preached to the householder was of ten some. The non-Aryans were probably out-numbering the Aryans, and they were anixous to have a strong and large army. Under these circumstances it would have been a suicidal policy to encourage the revival of the absolute custom of Sati or to prohibit remarriage of widows. Society came to the definite conclusion that its vital interests demanded that the custom of Sati should be interdicted, and that widows should be allowed and encouraged to remarry and multiply the stock.[20]

Whatever the reasons may have been, it is undisputed that the Sati custom had gone out of vogue among the Aryans at the time they had entered India. We find no traces of it whatsoever down to 400 B.C. The Brahmin literature (1500 B.C.-700 B.C.) is silent about it. The Grihyasutras (600

B.C.-300 B.C.) describe numerous rituals and sacraments, but the custom of Sati does not figure among them. From the details of the funeral ritual and procedure given in time, we find that the widow was to be brought back from the funeral pyre either by her husband's brother or disciple, or by an old trusted servant.[21] From the *Taittiriya Aranyaka* was find that while returning from the funeral pure, the widow took away from her husband's hand objects like bow, gold, jewels, etc. which were burnt along with the widow in an earlier age. A hope was then expressed that the widow and her relatives would lead a happy and prosperous life.[22] It is clear that the custom of Sati had died down long ago.

The Buddhist literature does not contain any specific references to Sati. If it had existed in the days of the Buddha, one feels certain that he would have started a vehement crusade against it. He, who opposed sacrifices to gods, because dumb animals were killed therein, would certainly have been exasperated by a custom which entailed the burning of human beings alive. Widows were instead welcomed as nuns if they so chose. Some of the votive inscriptions at Buddhist stupas record donations by widows. The later Jaina muni could die by slow starvation. This concession prevented the Jainas from opposing other forms of religions suicide. However, judging by the large number of Jaina widows who became nuns, it is evident that although some[23] might have become satis, this was not the prevailing custom was not popular upto 500 B.C. even in the Kshatriya circles.

We have no reference to this practice either in Kautilya or Megasthenese, in the Dharmasutras or in the early Smritis like Manu's or Yajnavalkya's, though we have in them an elaborate discussion of the duties of widows as well as suicides.

The first literacy references to the custom of Sati is provided by the *Mahabharata,* a major portion of which was composed it labour 300 B.C. The most important case is that of Madri, the queen of Pandu. However, the assembled sages try their best to dissuade her from her resolve. Madri, however, is unmoved by their arguments and says that she is determined to die with her lord, because *(a)* she was the cause of his death, *(b)* she might find it difficult to treat evenly her sons and stepsons.[24] No argument of any religious merit is assigned by her or by anybody else.

The question of honour was not centrally involved as Pandu died an ignoble death, unable to contain his lust tor Madri and she gives this as one of the reasons why she should follow her husband into the realms of Yama. Faithfulness in this situation seems theoretical, since both wives of Pandu had conceived sons from various other males, albeit deities, Pandu not being in a position to father a child. Madri is not deified either like later Satis.[25] Wheeler[26] has, however, compared Madri's case with that of the Thracian practice in which wives of a man contested among themselves to prove that she was the best loved wife and hence the honour of immolating herself with her husband should be conferred on her. Madri did the same with Kunti and urged the circumstances of his death as a proof that she was the best-beloved and then mounted the funeral pyre.[27]

Wheeler, expresses his doubt about the case of Madri. He writes: "The legend, however, respecting the Sati of Madri is not altogether without suspicion, inasmuch as it is the only instance recorded in connection with the family of Bharat".[28] Neither the widow of Santanu nor the widows of Vichitravirya perished upon the funeral pure. The old king Santanu was dead and his youthful queen appears to have lived many years after him as a matron and Queen mother. It may be that Madri was from the frontier areas and there was a practice in warlike tribes there to immolate herself with the dead husband.[29]

The first foreign account of Sati is furnished by the Greeks. In 316 B.C. the Hindu general Keteus died in the battle between Antigones and Eumenes.[30] He had two wives; the elder one was enceinte. Both of them were eager to commit sati but the elder one was prevented from doing so on account of her condition, at which the elder wife went away lamenting, with the band about her head rent, and tearing her hair, as if tidings of some great disaster had been brought her and the other departed, exultant at her victory, to the pyre, crowned with fillets by the women who belonged to her and decked out splendidly as for a wedding.[31] She was escorted by her kinsfolk who chanted a song in praise of her virtue. When she came near the pyre, she took off her adornments and distributed them to her familiars and friends, leaving a memorial for herself, as it were, to those who had loved her. Her adornments consisted of a multitude of rings on her hands, set with precious gems of diverse colours, about her head golden stars not few, variegated with different sorts of stones, and about her neck a multitude of necklaces, each a little larger than the one about it. In conclusion, she said farewell to her familiars and was helped by her brother onto the pyre, and there, to the admiration of the crowd which had gathered together for the spectacle, she ended her life in heroic fashion. Before the pyre was kindled, the whole army in battle array marched round it thrice. She meanwhile lay down beside her husband, and as the fire seized her no sound of weakness escaped her lips. The spectators were moved, some to pity and some to exuberant praise. But some of the Greeks present found fault with such customs as savage and inhuman.

The Greeks also had a "theory to account for the custom".[32] This theory was that the custom was designed to dissuade wives from poisoning their husbands.[33]

Thus it appears that the Greeks had mixed reactions about Sati. It was a mix of admiration for the heroic element and condemnation for the savage element in the rite; and speculation about the origin of the rite. These basic reactions cropped up time and again as westerners confronted the Sati rite.

The first epigraphical evidence is provided but he Eran posthumous inscription of Goparaja of 510 A.D. Goparaja was killed in the battle with the Hunas and his wife mounted the funeral pyre of her husband.[34]

The first canonical reference is provided by *Visnudharmasutra*. It declares: "On her husband's death the widow should observe celibacy or should ascend the funeral pyre after him."[35] Here offers an option, a widow may resort to either of the two paths.

The latest reported case of Sati has come from Deorala (Rajasthan) in 1987 where a young Rajput lady committed Sati.

Thus for almost two thousand five hundred years the practice has continued in India. Sometimes a few stray cased are reported but in the medieval period it became more popular. Earlier it was purely voluntary, later compulsion began to be exercised. It was more popular in Kashmir and Rajputana during the medieval times. In 18th and 19th Century it was more popular in Bengal. Earlier Kings and nobbles preferred it and hence it was more popular in Rajput circles. Later on Brahmins also followed it. Still later some Sudras also initiated the upper castes.

Sati is an amalgam of two distinct concepts -- religious self-immolation and burning of widows. Both were common enough among many ancient tribes and primitive religious communities. But Indians or rather the Hindus, got singled out for understandable reasons. It has been practised in India, sporadically, over the longest period of time. There is no other society where it was practised by various social groups for different reasons at various points in time and where the controversy over whether or not it should be practised was so clearly articulated over many centuries. Because of this, in India, it underwent changes of meaning as well as degree of acceptance.

"Its origin is generally traced to the subordination of women in patriarchal society and this seems to be the form it takes in more recent times. But in searching for origins it might be as well, to consider other situations which prevailed in India. The notion of bride price, for example, can suggest in some situations the purchase of a woman, the logical termination of which may have been the requirement of her dying together with her husband, although this is not typical of bride-price. But perhaps a more acceptable explanation may relate to societies changing their systems of kingship and inheritance. In some circumstances the wife would be an olian in the early stages of change. Control over female sexuality would be a further reason".[36] There is no simple explanation for the origin of the custom. It is said to be a symbol of aristocratic status associated with many early societies. The practice may have originated among societies in flux and become customary among those holding property such as the families of chiefs and kshatriyas. Once it was established as a custom associated with the Kshatriyas it would continue to be so among those claiming Kshatriya status as well.

Amongst the Aryans, a widow was made over to a Kinsman (brother or other male relative) of the deceased husband; amongst the Scythians a favourite widow or concubine was sent to accompany the dead man. The Aryan custom of Niyoga and widow marriage fell into disuse amongst the twice-born castes and were superseded by the later custom of Sati. Still the fact, that traces of the rite are to be found in tribes dwelling in India during the vedic period, seems to justify an investigation of those instinctive passions under which it eventually merged into Brahmanical law.

Two ideas are involved in the later Brahmanical rite which find no expression in the early Scythic form, namely, that the act was voluntary on the part of the widow, and that it was associated with a well-grounded belief in the immortality of the soul. The widow, indeed, entered the fire with a profound conviction that she would thereby rejoin her husband in abode of bliss.[37]

The Thracians had a similar custom, except that the widow was not burnt, but slaughtered at the grave of her dead husband by her next of kin; and it is curious to note that the doctrine of the immortality of the soul had been promulgated amongst the Thracians at an early period by a religious teacher named Zaloxis. A further reference to the working of the state has superseded the old crude idea of wandering ghosts, and becomes the unquestioned faith of the people, a latent desire exists in every wedded pair who have truly lived and loved together, to accompany each other to the tomb; and this desire is stronger in the wife to whom by common consent a larger measure of delicacy and sentiment is awarded.

"In India this desire appears to have been brought into play during that phase of civilization when sentiment begins to triumph over materialism; when the husband shuddered at the knowledge that after his widow would be transferred to his kinsmen, and the loving wife revolted at the idea of being made over to some individual who might already have had a wife of his own".[38]

There are also exceptional circumstances which would lead to an extension of the rite of Sati. The precautions to be taken by a King against being poisoned by a female, were rendered unnecessary when the female was condemned to enter the fire after the death of her master, and when the prolonged existence of a king was a point of paramount importance to every wife and concubine in his harem. Again, the unprotected state in which widows receive as mere dependents in the family, must have driven many a distracted women to enter the fire and follow the soul of a loving husband. In a still later age, when the sati became associated with the Brahmanical religion, and was glorified as an act which conferred lasting fame on the wife, and everlasting happiness on herself and her husband, it is not surprising that the rite should have become general throughout India. In that terrible hour which succeeds a the death of a beloved husband, when the reason is crazed with grief, and the harem is filled with weeping and wailing, it is easy to understand that a widow would prefer a glorious death before a thousand spectators, and immediate reunion with a deceased husband, to a life of degradation, in which every pleasure would be denied her, and her very presence would be regarded as an evil omen. The original distinction between the Scythian and Aryan usage is thus obvious. The Scythians slaughtered a living female to enable her to accompany the dead man; the Aryans placed the widow in charge of the new head of the family. Both usage found expression among the Rajputs. The dead man was burnt according to the Aryan fashion; but the living widow was burnt with him in order that she might accompany her husband to the world of spirits. The rite os Sati, as practised by the Rajputs, may thus be described as a Scythian usage modified by Aryan culture.[39] The bodies, dead and living, were no longer buried, but burned. The female was no longer slaughtered as an unwilling victim to the selfish sensuality of a barbarian. On the contrary, she was the widow of a high souled Rajput; the reflex of his chivalrous devotion; prepared to perish with him in order that she might accompany her deceased lord to a heaven of felicity. The Scythian Sati was further modified by the Aryan worship of fire and the Sun. Agni or fire was the purifying deity. She was not only the domestic soggess of the household, but also the divine messenger that carried the sacrifice to the gods; the purifying flame that bore away the widow and her lord to the mansions of the Sun. In this manner the horrible rite, so revolting to civilization and humanity, was imbued with an element of the religion of affections.[40] It elevated the helpless concubine into a self-sacrificing heroine; the distracted widow into a joyful and triumph and bride. The future of the bereaved woman was no longer a vista of shame and sorrow. She ascended the pyre as the chariot of fire which was to carry her away to the arms of her glorified bridegroom in the realms of bliss.

Such was the rite which the Rajput and the Brahman carried to nearly every quarter of India. It was the expression of the highest conjugal faction combined with the lowest state of female degradation. The unfortunate widow had no way to escape for a joyless life of servitude, excepting by the most horrible sacrifices. The honour of the family depended upon the heroism of the woman; and the widow was too often condemned to the point of martyrdom when the heroism was altogether wanting. The victim was stupefied with drugs, and adorned as a burnt offering. She was led by the Brahmans to the pyre form which flight was impossible. The timber was set on fire by the nearest kinsman, and often by her own son, amidst the deafening noise of drums, and the cries of an excited throng.

There is still a deeper level of explanation of Sati which needs to be adumbrated here. Between the end of the Vedic period and 12th Century A.D., the idea seemed to have gained ground that the husband should have exclusive and total control over his wife's sexuality. Pre-pubertal marriage was the surest way to make certain of it. Pre-pubertal marriage also transferred the responsibility for safeguarding the girl's sexuality from her male kin in her natal family to her husband and his agnates. Once married, total faithfulness was expected of the wife, and this was attempted to be assured by the deification of the husband. "Total control over her sexuality was not only for the duration of the marriage; it extend to the pre- and post-marital periods, absurd as it may seem to outsiders".[41] Virginity in brides was ensured by pre-pubertal, and frequently, child marriages, while celibacy was required of the widow. She was disfigured by having her head shaved, and by forbidding to her the symbols of the happy and auspicious state of sumanglihood, and her activities were restricted to the kitchen and to ritual. She was condemned to perpetual mourning, as it were, and she became a symbol of inauspiciousness and ill-luck. The death of her husband was attributed to the sins she had committee in a previous birth. The widow who decided to commit sati was, on the contrary, auspicious, and she was dressed as a bride for her last journey. He martyrdom brought good reputation and good luck other kinsfolk and to her village. In some parts of India, memorial stones were erected to Satis.

While the widow and Sati were treated so radically differently, the central idea in both the cases was the assertion of the dead husband's total control over the wife's sexuality. The wife, on the other hand, had no such exclusive right over the husband's sexuality. Not only was a widower not required to burn himself on his dead wife's general pyre, he was urged to marry soon. Even during the life-time of her wife he could marry another woman in many cases. This one-sidedness is really the key to the relationship between husband and wife in India.

As we have seen, the earliest notices of Sati amongst the Hindus are to be found in the Greek accounts of the expedition of Alexander in the 4th Century B.C. The rite as there said to have been adopted as a check upon the women, who occasionally put a husband to death for the sake of a younger lover.[42] The Greek story may have been based on authentic tradition. In the age of Aryan or Rajput conquest, a captive princess often became the unwilling wife of her conqueror; and under such circumstances might be tempted to revenge the affront by poison or the dagger.[43]

But the statement of Strabo does not harmonize with the assertion that the marriages were based on mutual affection. Sati might have proved a check to poison in days when girls were compelled to accept old men as their husbands; but nothing was to be feared form loving wives. The latter, however, obeyed the ordinance, for being imbued with an unquestioning faith that they would thereby join their husbands in a heaven of felicity.[44] Abbe J.A. Dubois[45] also does not accept the theory put forward by the Greeks. He writes: "As for myself, I have been unable, either in the writings of Hindu authors or in my free and familiar intercourse with many persons well versed in the manners and customs of the country, to discover any justification for either of these two theories" that this practice originated primarily either from the jealousy of husbands or from their fear that their discontented wives might seek to get rid of them by poison. "Surely the lot of a wife, even when she is doomed to suffer wrong at the hands of a cruel and immoral husband, if far preferable to that of a widow, to whom all hope of a remarriage under happier conditions is forbidden. It is hardly likely, indeed that Hindu women would go to the length of committing a crime which must render their lot much worse than before!".

REFERENCES

1. A.S. Altekar, *The Position of Women in Hindu Civilization,* (Delhi: Motilal Banarasi Dass, 1962), p. 116.
2. P.V. Kane, *History of Dharmasastra,* Vol. II, Part I (Poona: Bhandarkar Oriental Research Institute, 1941), p. 625.
3. Die Frau, pp. 56, 82-83.
   Schrader, *Prehistoric Antiquities of the Aryan People* (London: 1890), p. 391;
   Westermarck, *Origin and Development of Moral Ideas,* Vol. I, pp. 472-76 (Pub. 1906).
4. Herodotus, IV, 71. Quoted in J. Talboys Wheeler, *India of the Vedic Age* (Delhi, Cosmo Publications, 19730, p. 69.
5. Herodotus, V, 5.
6. Westermarck, *op. cit.,* pp. 247ff.; Also see *Encyclopaedia of Religion and Ethics,* Vol. XII, New York, 1921, p. 27.
7. Quoted in *Encyclopaedia of Religion and Ethics,* Vol. XII, pp. 27ff.
8. Tawney: *Kathasaritsagara,* Vol. IV, Bombay, 1903. Terminal Essay on Suttee by Penzer.
9. Westermarck, *op. cit.,* Vol. II, p. 242.
10. W.M. Flinders Petric, *Religious life in Ancient Greece,* p. 391.
11. Upendra Thakur, *THe History of Suicide in India* (Delhi: Munshi Ram Manohar Lal, 1963), p. 127.
12. A.S. Altekar, *op. cit.,* pp. 116-17.
13. D.D. Kosambi, *Myth and Reality* (Bombay: Popular Prakashan, 1962), pp. 80-81.
14. D.D. Kosambi, *The Culture and Civilization of Ancient India in Historical Outline* (Delhi: Vikas, 1975), p. 119.
15. Allchin, Bridget and Raymond, *The Birth of Indian Civilization,* 1968, p. 139.
16. इयं नारी पतिलोकं वृणाना निपद्यते उपत्वा मत्य प्रेतम् ।
   धर्म पुराणमनुपालयनी तस्य प्रजां द्रविणं चह द्यत ।।
   - A.V., XVIII, 2, 1.

17. A.S. Altekar, *op. cit.*, p. 118.
18. *Ibid.*, pp. 338-39.
19. *Ibid.*, p. 342.
20. *Ibid.*, pp. 342-43.
21. तामुत्यापयेद्वेवरः पतिस्थानीयांऽनोवासी जरद्धासो वा 'उदीर्ष्व नार्यभि जीवलोकम्' इति।

    - *Apastamba Grihyasutra*, IV, 2, 18.
22. धनुर्हस्तादाददाना मृतस्य श्रियेः ब्रह्मणे तेजसे बलाय।

    अत्रैव त्वमिह वयं सुशेवा विश्वाः तृधोऽभिजातीर्जयेम।।
    - *Taittiriya Aranyaka*, VI, 1.
23. *Epigraphia carnatica*, Vol. VIII, Sorab Nos. 106 & 261, dated 1376 and 1408 resepectively.
24. अहमेवानुयास्यामि भर्तारमपलापिनम्।

    न हि तृप्तास्मि कामानां ज्येष्ठा मामनुयन्यताम्।।
    वर्तेयं न समां वृत्रिं जात्वहं न सतेष तु।
    - *Mahabharat*, I, 138, 71-72.
25. Romila Thapar, "In History", *Seminar*, February 1988, pp. 17-18.
26. J. Talboys Wheeler, *India of the Vedic Age* (Delhi: Cosmo Publications, 1973), pp. 69-70.
27. तत्रेनं चिताग्निस्थं माद्रो समन्वारूरोह।

    - *Mbh*, Adi, 95, 65.
28. Wheeler, *op. cit.*, p. 70.
29. For details of other cases of the *Mahabharata* see Chapter on "Sati in Literature" of this thesis.
30. N.M. Penzer, ed., *The Ocean of Story*, Vol. IV, (London: Chas. J. Sawyer, 1925), p. 261; A.S. Altekar, *op. cit.*, 122.
31. R.C. Majumdar, ed., *The Age of Imperial Unity* (Bombay: Bhartiya Vidya Bhawan, 1953), pp. 567-68.
32. N.M. Penzer, *op. cit.*, p. 262.
33. Edward Thompson, *Suttee* (London: George Allen & Unwin, 1928), p. 44.
34. *Fleet*, C.I.I., Vol. III, p. 91.
35. "मृते भर्तरि ब्रह्वर्य तदन्वारोहणं वा"

Quoted by the *Mitakshara* on *Yajnavalkyasmrti,* I, 86.

36. Romila Thapar, *op. cit.*, p. 15.
37. James Talboys Wheeler, *Ancient and Hindu India: The Brahmanic Period* (Calcutta: Punthi Pustak, 1961), p. 168.
38. *Ibid.*, p. 168.
39. J. Talboys Wheeler, *India from the Earliest Ages* (Delhi: Cosmo Publications, 1973), p. 89.
40. *Ibid.*, p. 90.
41. M.N. Srinivas, Foreword to Arvind Sharma, *Sati,* (Delhi: Motilal Banarsi Dass, 1988), p. XII.
42. Strabo, India, Sect, 30.
43. J. Talboys Wheeler, *India from the Earliest Ages, op. cit.*, fn p. 70.
44. *Ibid.*, fn. 31 on p. 173.
45. Abbe J.A. Dubois, *Hindu Manners, Customs and Ceremonies* (Oxford: Clarendon Press, 1953), p. 358.

3

The Scriptural Sanction for Sati

We have already seen that the custom of Sati was not prevalent during the Vedic period. Even if the Indo-Aryans had some such practice before coming to India, the practice fell in disuse due to political and religious circumstances. In fact, the widow was allowed *niyoga* and remarriage in the Vedic period. The *Atharvaveda* treats the practice of Sati as ancient religion which was discarded when the Aryans entered India.

However, when the practice of Sati came under attack at the hands of Christian missionaries and Hindu reformers in the early decades of the 19th Century, efforts were made to defend it on scriptural grounds. In this connection some verses from the Vedas were cited to support the rite of Sati. In this chapter we, therefore, propose to examine the scriptural evidence in support of Sati.

Rg Veda, X, 18, 7-8[1] have been cited to support the practice of Sati in the Vedic age. According to Apararka, it is these verses "which render self-immolation free from the sin of suicide"[2] and are thus to be associated with Sati. But P.V. Kane, after examining the context in which these verses appear, points out:

> "The two verses are employed by the Baudhayana - *Pitrmedha Sutra* in the funeral rites, the first to be repeated when the wife is made to sit near the corpse and the next for making her rise. It is to be noted

that Baud directs that the corpse is placed on the funeral pile after the wife is made to rise from the vicinity of the corpse; while the *Brhad-Devata* appears to suggest that the wife ascends the funeral pile after the corpse is placed there on and then the younger brother forbids her with the verse 'udirsva and C." But the *Brhaddevata* does not mean that the wife burden herself on their funeral pyre and the brother-in-law contents herself with only repeating a verse to dissuade her. The *Rgvidhana (III, 8, 4,)* says that the brother-in-law should call back the wife of his sonless brother when she is about to ascend the funeral pyre for procreating a son on her with Rg. X, 18.8. It appears that the verse Rg., X, 18, 8 symbolically describes what even in the days of the *Rgveda* was probably only a tradition viz. that in hoary antiquity a wife burnt herself with her husband. In the times of the *Rgveda* this practice had altogether ceased, but a symbolical imitation of it had come into vogue, viz. that the wife lay near the corpse in the cement and then she was asked to get up and was told that by following her husband to the very doors of death she had fulfilled all that was expected of her and that she should return. The same idea is referred to by the verse 'iyam-nari', but the latter had appears to refer to the practice of *niyoga* when it calls upon the departed to bestow on the wife offspring and wealth. It is possible to argue that *Rg* x, 18, 8 also impliedly has niyoga in view. But both these verses do not expressly refer to the practice of Sati at all.[3]

Earlier, H.H. Wilson, wrote an article in the *Journal of the Royal Asiatic Society of Great Britain and Ireland*[4] on the supposed authority for the burning of Hindu widows, and on the funeral ceremonies of the Hindus generally. He distinctly shows that sacred books contain no authority whatever for the performance of widows, obviously implying that the death of the wife was never supposed to accompany that of the husband. To quote the words of Prof. Wilson:

> "In the lecture on the Vedas which I read during our last session I had occasion to notice some very remarkable passages in one of the *Suktas,* or hymns of the *Rg,* relating to the disposal of the dead, and especially to the burning of widows, for which the hymn in question was always cited as authority. I stated then that the text quoted for that purpose had a totally different tendency,..... I added, however, that I had not had time to consider the passage with that care which they required, and that I communicated only the results of my first impressions. I have since examined the passages more deliberately, and propose now to offer to the society the conclusions which I have deliberately formed; namely, that the text of the *RgVeda* cited as authority for the burning of widows enjoins the very contrary, and directs them to remain in the world....

The author of the *Grhyasutra* Asvalayana furnishes further proof of what is meant, as he specifies the person who is to address the stanza of the widow, placed on the north of her deceased husband's head, and who is to be her husband's brother, or a fellow-student or an old servant, and who, having thus spoken to her, is to take her away. The authority of the Sutras is a little inferior to that of the Veda; and here, therefore, we have additional and incontestable proof, that the *RgVeda* does not authorise the practice of burning of the widow".

Not only Aparарka, the medieval commentator, but even Max Muller, the modern scholar, sees a connection between *Rg Veda* X, 18, 7 and the practice of Sati though for different reasons. The verse translates as follows:

> Let these women, who are not widows and who have good husbands, sit down with clarified butter used as collyrium; may the wives who are tearless, free

from disease and wearing fine jewels (or clothes) occupy the seat in front (first).[5]

Charles Rockwell Lanman remarks thus on the role this stanza has played in the controversy over Sati.

From Muller's Essay on *Comparative Mythology, Chips,* ii, 34 for *Selected Essays,* Vol. I, (ed. of 1881), p. 333f, it would appear that the seventh stanza of our hymn had played a great role in Hindu history. At any rate, this idea is current, and seems traceable to the Essay. Here it is stated that the stanza was purposely falsified by an unscrupulous priesthood, and that a garbled version of it, reading *agneh* for *agre* was directly responsible for sacrifice of thousands of innocent lives. That the author is in error on these points is argued with great detail by Fitzedward Hall, *JRAS,* Ns. III. 183-192. He shows that a misreading can be traced to Raghunandana (a. 1500 A.D., and no further; and that Suttee was deemed to be amply justified by warrants other than those of the Vedic *Samhita,* which was by no means the ultimate appeal for the medieval Hindu.[6]

In this context the remarks made by both Max Muller and Kaegi on the role of brahmanas in the commission of Sati seem to show a lack of historical awareness of this change. On the alteration of *agre* into *agne* in *Rgveda* X 18, 7, Max Muller remarks: This is perhaps the most flagrant instance of what can be done by an unscrupulous priesthood. Here have thousands of lives been sacrificed, and a practical rebellion threatened on the authority of a passage which was mangled, mistranslated and misapplied".[7]

Kaegi's comment is also on the same lines. He remarks: "The well-known custom of burning of widows for thousands of years demanded by the Brahmanas, is no where evidenced in the *Rgveda;* only by palpable falsification of a hymn has the existence of the custom been forcibly put into the texts which, on the contrary, prove directly the opposite, i.e. the return of the widow from her husband's corpse into a happy life and her remarriage".[8]

According to A.S. Altekar "even when the last word is

changed into *agneh,* it is only a forced construction that can detect in this stanza a reference to the widow immolation".[9]

On the alleged role of Raghunandana in instituting the change, Kane holds, "The *Suddhitattva* as pointed is corrupt but it appears that it read the last quarter of *Rg* X, 18, 7 as *'arohantu jalayonim-agne* (let them ascend the watery seat or origin, 0 fire;) meaning probably 'may fire be to them as cool as water'. Some writers have charged the brahmana priesthood (or Raghunandana) with having purposely changed the reading of the Verse *Rg* X, 18, 7 in order to make it suit the rite of immolating oneself in fire (i.e.*'agne'* or *'agneh'* was substituted for agre). But this charge is not sustainable. That the verse *RG* X 18, 7 as it actually is, was held to refer to widow burning centuries before Raghunandana follows from the fact that even the Brahmapurana and Apararka (quoted above on p. 628) take it in that sense. It was therefore not necessary to alter the reading. Further, even if some priests or Raghunandana had changed it, that fact would have been detected in no time, as in those days there were thousands of people who knew every syllable of the *RgVeda* by heart. Therefore it must be admitted that either the mss. are corrupt or Raghunandana committed an innocent slip. That mantra was not addressed to widows at all, but to ladies of the deceased man's household whose husbands were living and the *Grhyasutra* of Asv. made use of it with that meaning. Raghunandana, a profound student of *dharmasastras* and *smrties* (and often styled *Smarta-bhattacarya*), could not have been ignorant of what ASV. said".[10]

Commenting on the disposal of the dead in the Vedic period, A.A. Macdonell says:

> "The dead man was provided with ornaments and clothing for use in the next life; the object of the custom being still understood in the *Veda* (AV. XVIII, 4. 31). Traces even survive (*RV.* X, 18, 8-9), which indicate that his widows and his weapons were once burnt with the body of the husband".[11]

Elsewhere he seems to refer to *RgVeda* X, 18, 8-9 and *Atharvaveda* XVIII, 3, 1 when he says, "In conformity with a custom provided with ornaments and clothing for use in the future life. The fact that in the funeral obsequies of the *RgVeda* the widow lies down beside the body of her deceased husband and his bow is removed form the dead man's hand, shows that both were in earlier times burnt with his body to accompany him to the next world, and a vase of the *Atharva-veda* calls the dying of the widow within that this was a very primitive practice widely prevailing at the funerals of military chiefs, and it can be proved to go back to the Indo-European age."[12]

Bhagwat Saran Upadhyaya, after citing these passages from A.A. Macdonell, remarks,

These remarks are based on a verse of the *RgVeda* which reads as follows: "Rise, come unto the world of life, O Woman; come, he is lifeless by whose side thou liest". But this part of the verse is soon followed up by the next line which gives the widow immediately away in marriage to the man who woes her. It reads: "Wifehood with this thy husband was the portion who took thy hand and wooed thee as a lover". The allusion to the lying down of the widow by the side of the remains of her husband's body contained in the earlier part of the verse may be taken to be referring to a feature of the earlier times when widows may have been burnt along with the dead body of their husbands. There is actually a verse contained in the *Atharvaveda* which preserves such a custom of burning the widow and which it calls an ancient religious duty (*dharmam puranam*). It is probable that the ancient custom against which the *Atharvaveda* raises a banner of revolt on humanitarian grounds had already grown too old to be followed during the time which the *Rgveda* depicts. But although the old custom had been given up the rites of its occasion, it would seem, still persisted and the precession of unwidowed women to adorn the widow for the company of the dead husband became one to deck her as a new bride. The process must have become very mechanical and sad for it is hardly human to be changed form a widow to a bride immediately after the death of the nearest relative and supporter of a woman even in the gay conditions of the Rgvedic society."[13]

Raja Radhakant Deva relied on two passages[14] which he found in the Aukhya Sakha of the *Taittiriya Samhita* quoted in the 84th Anuvaka of the Narayaniya upanisad as the most explicit authority for widow burning. But Kane doubts the authenticity of the passages.[15] A.S. Altekar observes that the passages in question refer to "a prayer by a widow to god Fire that she was about to follow the *anugamana-vrata* or the sati custom and that she may be able to bear the ordeal and reap the promised reward. The *Narayaniya-upanisad* is however a late work, the passage from the Aukhya Sakha quoted in it is otherwise not known to us from any other source. We cannot therefore conclude from it that the Sati custom was recognised as a ritual in the Vedic period."[16]

According to A.C. Das,[17] the custom of self-immolation is referred to in the *Atharvaveda,* XVIII, 3,1.[18] This verse translates as follows:

> "This woman, choosing her husband's world, lies down *(nipad)* by thee that art departed, O mortal, continuing to keep her ancient duty *(dharma)*; to her assign thou here progeny and property."[19]

It shows that the funeral ritual of the Vedic age preserved some formalities reminiscent of the archaic custom of Sati. It shows that it was still customary for the widow to lie by the side of her husband's corpse on the funeral pryer; she was, however, asked to come down, and a prayer was offered that she should lead a prosperous life enjoying the bliss of children and wealth.[20]

But the next verse, XVIII, 3.2 is the same as the verse in RV, X, 18, 8 about which it has already been noticed and about which it may be reiterated that "the verse in consideration seems to be addressed by a priest to a wife who sat near the funeral pyre of her husband. Thus it proceeds:

> "Rise, come into the *world of life.* O Woman; Come, he is lifeless by whose side thou liest. Wifehood with this thy husband was thy portion, was took thy hand wooed thee as a lover." The word "Jivaloka" in the verse is certainly enough to support the view that a widow was not consigned to flames but brought back to the living world to lead her life as usual".[21]

Hence, while it is clear that the custom of Sati is alluded to in the Vedic Verses, it is equally clear that it was not practised during the Vedic period. As we have already seen, the Visnudharmasutra is the earliest Smrti literature to mention Sati. To quote P.V. Kane, "None of the Dharmasutras except Visnu contains any reference to Sati."[22] In fact when Visnu[23] says 'after the death of her husband, a woman should practise asceticism or mount the funeral pyre of her husband', he does not recommend it. He only mentions it as one of the options open to a widow. A.S. Altekar writes: "*Vishnusmriti* (c.100 A.D.) thinks the custom to be not illogical; it advanced the view that in spite of diversity of Karman, a widow can, though other relations cannot, go the way of the departed soul by dying after him".[24] The custom, however, was not yet regarded as a religious duty. Visnu himself does not recommend it; he merely mentions it. He is in fact one of the earliest writers to recognise the widow as an heir to her husband; he allows her to remarry also (17,43).[25]

According to Angiras, quoted by Apararka, "for all women there is no other duty except falling into the funeral pyre, when the husband dies".[26] Angiras, however, does not allow Brahman widow to mount the funeral pyre.

There are some verses drawn upon in common, which are found in *Parasara*[27] and *Brahmapurana (Gautami Mahatmya)*; and quoted in the *Mitaksara* commentary on *Yajnavalkya* 1.86 and by Apararka and the *Suddhitattva*. According to these verses:

Sankha and Angiras say 'she who follows her husband in death dwells in heaven for as many years as there are hair on the human body, viz. 3½ crores of years. Just as a snake charmer draws out snake from a hole by force, so such a woman draws her husband from wherever he may be and enjoys bliss together with him. In heaven she being solely devoted to her husband and praised by bevies of heavenly damsels sports with her husband for as long as fourteen Indras' rule.

Even if the husband be guilty of the murder of a brahmana, of a friend or be guilty of ingratitude, the wife who dies in fire clasping his body, purifies him of the sin. That woman, who ascends the funeral pyre when the husband dies, is equal to Arundhati in her character and is praised in heaven. As long as a woman does not burn herself in fire on the death of her husband she is never free from being born as a woman in successive births.[29]

Sukra leaves it to the choice of the widow herself, whether to follow her dead husband or to keep living in the world. In the latter case she was incessantly to worship gods, revere the memory of her husband and perform other regular penances.[30]

Harita says "that woman who follows her husband in death purifies three families, viz. of her father, or her mother and of her husband".[31]

The *Smrtimuktaphala* and *Madan Parijata* cite verses, also quoted in the *Mitaksara*, to the effect that the duty of *anvarohana* is common to the women of all castes from the brahmana to the candela provided they are not pregnant or they have no young children at the husband's death.[32]

A similar opinion has expressed by *Brhannardiya Purana* quoted in *Parasarmadhaviya*. It says that women before puberty, with small children, pregnancy and when they are in monthly course are not to mount the funeral pyre.[33] Brihaspati supports this view.[34]

Apastamba prescribes the *Prajapatya* penance for a woman who having first resolved to burn herself on the funeral pyre turns back from it at the last moment.[35]

The *Padmapurana* extols the custom to the sky, but expressly prohibits it to Brahmana women. It declares that any person, who will be guilty of helping a Brahmana widow to the funeral pyre, will be guilty of the dreadful and unatonable sin of the murder of a Brahmana.[36]

Harita is positively against the practice being resorted to by Brahman ladies. In his opinion, they, burning themselves, obstruct even the souls of their husbands, from entering into heaven."[37] Several texts cited by Aparарka from Pathinasi, Angiras, Vyaghrapad forbid self-immolation by Brahmana widows.[38]

The *Veda-Vyasa Smrti,* however, advises a Brahmana widow to enter fire, clasping the dead body of her husband. In case, she does not, she should give up all luxuries and emaciate her body by austerities.[39]

This apparent contradiction of views regarding sati by Brahman widows was reconciled by commentators later on. Apararka (12th Century) in his comment on Yajnavalkya (1, 87) argues that "when death by mounting the funeral pyre of the husband was apparently prohibited to a Brahmana widow, what was meant was that she should not take the step merely under a temporary sense of overwhelming grief.[40]

Madhava (14th Century) in his comment on Parasara (IV, 31) argues that "the intention may be to interdict death by mounting a separate funeral pyre; a Brahman widow must always be burnt along with her husband's remains on the same pyre."[41]

The authors of digests explained away the passages forbidding the self-immolation of a Brahmana widow "by saying that they only prohibit self immolation by a brahmana widow on a funeral pyre different from that of her husband"[42] i.e. *Sahamarana* was permissible.

The criticism of Sati system by Medhatithi (On Manu, V, 157) where he compares it with *Syenayaga* and suicide and therefore *asastrya* and *adharma* was combated by the *Mitaksara* (on Yaj, 1, 86). It says that *Syenayaga* is no doubt undesirable and therefore *adharma,* but, that is so because the object of *Syenyaga* is injury to another. *Anugaman,* on the other hand, is not so; there the result promised is heaven which is a desirable result and which is enjoined by *Sruti* in such sentences as 'one should sacrifice a white goat to Vayu if one desires prosperity'. Similarly the *Smrti* about *anugaman* is not opposed to the *Sruti* quoted, the meaning of which is different; that *sruti* means, 'one should not waste one's life for securing heavenly bliss which is fluting and insignificant as compared with supreme bliss of Brahma knowledge. As a woman in *anumaran* desires only heaven, she is not doing anything contrary to the *sruti* texts. This reasoning of the Mitaksara looks like special pleading.

Aparaka, the Madan Parijat and Parasar Madhaviya follow the reasoning of the Mitaksara and add that the Vedic text about the allotted span of life is a general rule, while the *smrti* about *anumaran* is a special or exceptional *sastra* and hence there is no contradiction as the rule applies to all cases outside the excepted one.

Thus early *Smrti* literature does not support Sati, the later *smrtis* support it with some qualifications. Some *Smrtis* prohibit Brahman widows to commit satis, later it was held that they could mount the same pyre with her dead husband.

REFERENCES

1. इमा नारीरविधवाः सुपत्नीरांजनेन सर्पिषा संविशन्तु।
   अनश्रवोऽनमोवाः सुरत्ना आरोहन्तु जनयो योनिमग्रे।
   उदीर्स्व नार्यभि जीवलोकं गतासुमेतमुपशेष ऐहि।
   हस्तग्राभस्य विधि धीस्तवेदं पत्युर्जानित्वमयिसंवभूथ।
   RgVeda, X, 17, 7-8.
2. P.V. Kane, *op. cit.,* p. 628, fn. 1472.
3. *Ibid.,* pp. 618-19.
4. Quoted in *The Bombay Times* and *Journal of Commerce,* dated 9.12.1854, reprinted the *The Times of India,* sesquicentennial issue, Nov-Dec; 1988, p. 13.
5. P.V. Kane, *op. cit.,* p. 716.

6. Charbs Rockwell Lanmen, *A Sanskrit Reader,* Harvard University Press, 1971, pp. 382-83. Quoted in Arvind Sharma, *op. cit.,* p. 35.
7. Quoted by P. Thomas, *Indian Women Through the Ages* (London: Asia Publishing House, 1964), p. 234.
8. Quoted in Indira, *The Status of Women in Ancient India* (Delhi: Motilal Banarasidass, 1955), p. 116.
9. A.S. Altekar, *op. cit.,* p. 117.
10. P.V. Kane, *op. cit.,* p. 634.
11. A.A. Macdonell, *The Vedic Mythology* (Varanasi: Indological Book House, 1971), p. 167.
12. A.A. Macdonell, *A History of Sanskrit Literature* (London: William Heinemann, 1913), pp. 125-26.

    Quoted in Arvind Sharma, *op. cit., p. 36.*
13. Bhagwat Saran Upadhyaya, *Women in RgVeda* (Benaras: Nand Kishore & Bros., 1941), p. 97.
14. "अग्ने वुतानां व्रतपतिरसि पत्न्युगवव्रतं करिष्यामि तच्छेकय तन्मेराध्यताम् ! इह त्वा अग्ने नमसा विधेम सुवर्गस्य लोकस्य समेत्यै। जुषाणोडद्यहविषा जातवेदा विशामित्वा सत्वतो नयमा पत्युरन्ते। "
15. P.V. Kane, *op. cit.,* p. 625, fn. 1462.
16. A.S. Altekar *op. cit.,* pp. 117-18.
17. Indra, *op. cit.,* pp. 115-16.
18. इमं नारी पतिलोकं वृणानां निपद्यते उप मर्त्य प्रेतम्। धर्मं पुराणमनुपालयती तस्य प्रजां द्रविणं यह धत्र।।

    - *Atharvaveda,* XVIII, 3.1.
19. William Dwight Whitney, *Atharva-Veda-Samhita,* Vol. II, (Delhi: Motilal Banarasidass, 1971), p. 848.
20. A.S. Altekar, *op. cit.,* p. 118.
21. Indira, *op. cit.,* p. 116.
22. P.V. Kane, *op. cit.,* pp. 625-26.
23. 'मृते भर्तारि ब्रह्मचर्य तदन्वारोहनं वा'

    Quoted by the Mitakshra On *Yaj.,* 1, 86.
24. मृतोऽपि बान्धवः शक्तो नानुगन्तं प्रियं जनम्।
    जायार्वणं हि सर्वस्य याम्यः पन्था विरूध्यते।।
    - *Visnu,* 20, 36.

25. A.S. Altekar, *op. cit.*, pp. 122-23.

26. साध्वीनामिह नारीणामग्निप्रपतनादृते।
नान्यो धर्मोऽस्ति विज्ञयो मृते भर्तारि कुत्रचित्।।
मृतसानुगमनं नास्ति ब्राह्मणया ब्रह्शासनात।
इतरेषां तु वर्णानां स्त्रीधर्माय परः स्मृतः।।
Angiras Quoted by Apararka on *Yaj*, 1, 87.

27. IV, 32-33.

28. स्त्रीणावयं परोधर्मे यद्भर्तुरनुवेशनम्।
वेदे च विहितो मार्गः सर्वलोकेषु पूजितः।।
व्यालग्राही यथा व्यांलं बिलादूद्धरते ब्लात्।
एवं त्वानुगता नारी सह भर्त्ता दिवं ब्रजेत।।
तिस्त्रः कोटयोऽर्धकोटी च यानि रोमाणि मानुषे।
तावत्कालं वसेत्स्वर्गे भर्तारं याऽनुगच्छति।।
- *Brahnapurana, Gautamimahatmya* Chap. XI, 75-77.

29. तिस्त्रः कोट्योऽधर्मकोटी च यानि लोमानी मानुषे।
तावत्कालं वसेत्स्वर्ग भर्तारं यानुगच्छति।।
व्यालग्राही यथा सर्प बलादुद्धरते बिलात्।
तद्वदुद्धत्य सा नारी सहतैनैव मोदते।।
तत्र सा भतृर्परमा स्तुयमानाप्सरोगणेः।
क्रीड़ते पतिना सार्ध यावदिन्दाश्चतुर्दशा।।
ब्रह्मध्नो वा कृतध्नो वा मित्रध्नो वा भवेत्पतिः।
पुनात्य विधवा नारी समारोहेद्धुताशनम्।
सारून्धती समाचारा स्वर्गलोके महीयते।।
यावच्चाग्नो मृते पत्यो स्त्रीनात्मानं प्रदाहयेत।
तावन्न मुच्येत सा हि स्त्रीशरीरात्कथचंन्ने।।
Quoted in Mitaksara on *Yaj*, 1, 86; Also in Apararka and *Suddhitattva*.

30. *Sukra*, IV, 4, 28-29.

31. P.V. Kane, *op. cit.*, p. 631.

32. अयं च सर्वास्तां स्त्रीणामगर्भिव्यीनाम बालापत्यानामाचाण्डालं साधारणो धर्माः।

33. बालापत्याश्च गर्भिणयो अदुष्टऋतवस्तथा।
रजस्वला राजसुते नारीहन्ति चितां शुभे।।

34. बालसंवर्धनं व्यक्त्वा बालापत्या न गच्छति।
रजस्वला सूतिका च रक्षेग्दर्भं च गर्भिणी।।

Brhaspati Quoted by *Parasar Madhaviya & Suddhitattva.*

Defining a *Pativrata* woman Brhaspati says:

आर्तीर्ते मुदिते दृष्टा प्रोषिते मलिना कृशा। मृते म्रियेत या पत्यौ सा स्त्री शैया पतिव्रता।।

35. चितिभ्रष्टा तु या नारी मोहाद्विचालिता ततः।
प्राजापत्येन शुध्येतु तस्माद्वे पापकर्मणः।।
Apastamba quoted by Aparárka and *Suddhitattva.*

36. न ग्रीयते समं भर्त्रा ब्राह्मणी ब्रह्मशासनात्।
प्रवर्ज्यागतिमाप्नोति मरणादात्मघातिनो।।
नरोत्तम उवाच - सर्वासामेव जातीनां ब्राह्मणः शस्त्र उच्यते।
पुण्यं च द्विजमुख्येन अत्र किं वा विषर्ययः।।
भगवुवाच - ब्राह्मण्या साहसं कर्म नेव कार्य कदाचन।
निश्शेषेऽस्या वधं कृत्वा नरो ब्रह्मा भवेत्।।
Padmapurana, Sristikhanda, 49, 72-73.

37. Indra, *The Status of Women in Ancient India* (Delhi: Motilal Banarasidass, 1955), p. 119.

38. पेठिनसिः। मृतानुगमनं नाळत्र, ब्राह्मणया ब्रह्शासनात्।
इतरेषां तु वर्णानां स्त्रीधर्मोयं परः स्मृतः।।
अगिरा। या स्त्री ब्राह्मणजातीया मृतं पतिमनुव्रजेत्।
सा स्वर्ग मात्मघातेन नात्मानं न पतिं नयेत।।
व्याघ्रपात। न प्रियते समं भर्ता ब्राह्मणी शोकमोहिता। प्रवेज्यागतियाप्नोति मरणादात्मघातिनी।।
Quoted by Aparárka.

39. मृतं भर्तारमादाय ब्राह्मणी वडिमाविशेत्।
जीवन्ती चेत्यवतकेश तपसा शोभपयेद्वपुः।।
- *Vedavyas Smrti,* II, 53.

40. तस्माद्विधितः प्रवर्तमानाया ब्राह्मण्या अनुगमा-
न्निषेधो न विद्यते। शोकादिप्रवृतयास्तु विद्यते रव।
- apararka on *Yaj,* 1, 87.

41. अस्य निषधस्य पृथक चिति निषेधत्वात्।
अत एवोश्नाः। पृथकियति समोरूह्य न विप्रा गन्तुमर्हति।
Madhava on *Parasara,* IV, 31.

42. P.V. Kane, *op. cit.*, p. 627.

4

Sati in Literature

We begin to find references to Sati in literature from about 300 B.C. We have already discussed the Sati of Madri in a previous Chapter. This is the only instance of Sati recorded in connection with the family of Bharat. Neither the widow of Santanu nor those of Vichitravirya perished on the funeral pyre. We have scores of instances of widows surviving their husbands. The wives of Drona, Abhimanyu and Ghatotkacha did not become Satis. There were thousands of Yadava widows who survived their husbands and accompanied Arjuna to Hastinapur. We have also the spectacle of hundreds and thousands of dead heroes being burnt along with their costumes, weapons and chariots; in not a single case, however, do we find a widow burning herself along with the remains of her husband. The epic itself states that all the widows of the fallen heroes remained behind and offered them funeral ablations.

We have a reference in Virat Parva where Draupadi is being forced to immolate with Kichaka.[1] This requires some detailed discussion.

The commander of the forces of King Virata fell in love with the waiting maid of the queen, who was his sister. He asked his sister to send the maid to his house, which was accordingly done; but the maid refused to listen to his proposals, being in fact the wife of the Pandavas in disguise. Subsequently the maid feigned consent, and agreed to meet him, but sent one of her husbands in her place. The lover, instead of meeting a mistress, found himself at the mercy of her husband who eventually pommelled him to death. In the morning there was a great uproar amongst the people, and the whole city was in commotion. The bretheren of Kichaka hastened to the spot and saw the dead body. They desired to take it away to the cremation ground. When they saw all the women of the palace gathered together, their eyes fell on Draupadi, and they said to one another. "This is the woman on whose account our brother has been murdered. We cannot kill her, because it is not proper to kill a woman: let us then burn her with the dead body of Kichaka, and, since he died out of love for her, let him espouse her in the world of ghosts."[2] They then went to the King and expressed their wish to burn the waiting-maid along with Kichaka. The King was in awe of his wife's bretheren and dared not forbid them. So they seized Draupadi by force, and bound her with cords and threw her on the bier of Kichaka, and went out of the city to burn her alive together with the dead body. Draupadi, seeing that her life was in mortal peril, shrieked and screamed in piteous tones and the air was filled with her cries. Ultimately Bhima rescued her killing the bretheren of Kichaka.

The climax of the narrative is reached when the bretheren of Kichaka seized the waiting-maid, and prepared to burn her upon the funeral pyre with the body of the dead man. This barbarous proceeding had no connection with the later Brahmanical idea of self-sacrifice on the part of a widow in the expectation of rejoining her deceased lord. It originated rather in the desire of the nearest relatives of the dead man that he should enjoy in death the society of the woman whom he had most loved in life. In such cases the willingness or otherwise of the unfortunate victims would be wholly ignored; and their murder would be a scene too painful to contemplate.[3] Indeed it is almost possible to sympathise in the momentary delirium which impels a poor widow to throw herself upon the pyre in the full expectation of enjoying everlasting bliss with her beloved husband in the realms of paradise. But the idea of putting an unhappy female to death, merely because she had unwillingly raised the desires of a voluptuary, is one upon which the mind can scarcely care to dwell. The distinction seems to be fully apprehended by a Hindu audience. Any interference in a Brahmanical Sati would have been regarded with a peculiar horror, while in the present instance the sympathies are all insisted in favour of the giant cook (Bhima) who rescues Draupadi from the burning pyre.

The idea of forcibly burning the waiting-maid with the dead body of Kichaka to avenge his death and to solace the ghost of the deceased with her society in the world of spirits is, perhaps, not Aryan but Scythian. According to Herodotus,[4] the Scythians were accustomed on the death of a king to strangle one of his concubines, and bury her willingness or otherwise". It may be therefore inferred from these data that Raja Virata was the chieftain of a Scythian tribe, which had encamped in the neighbourhood of an Aryan settlement".[5] Thus this was not a case of Sati.

From the Mausala-Parva we learn that four wives of Vasudeo—Devaki, Bhadra, Rohini and Madira—burnt themselves with him.[6] Similarly, Rukumini, Gandhari, Sahya, Haimavati and Jambavati ascended the funeral pyre of Krishna and Satyabhama retired to forest for practising penance.[7]

The *Mahabharata* also furnishes us with an interesting story. It describes how a *Kapoti (female* pigeon) entered fire on the death of her husband.[8] It should be noted that a very similar story has been mentioned in *Brahma Puruna*.[9] Hence it may be an interpolation. The Santi Parva is a later addition to the *Mahabharata*.

Thus the *Mahabharat* provides a few cases of Sati. It was not very popular. It was optional. Widows could practise austerity or mount the funeral pyre. Only a beginning was being made at that time.

In the original portion of the *Ramayan* there is no case

of Sati. The wives of Dasratha or Ravana do not mount the funeral pyres of their husbands. In the Uttar Kanda of the *Ramayan*[10] we find Vedvati's mother entering fire after being molested by Ravana. But this is a case of suicide and not of Sati. Moreover, "this story is more legendary than historical and the book where it occurs is admittedly a later addition."[11] We also find that when Ravana by means of his magic raised before the yes of Sita the illusion of the fall of Rama, Sita expressed the wish to be burnt along with her husband.[12] This passage also is probably a later interpolation.[13]

In the *Puranas* we find some cases of Sati. According to the *Padmapurana*[14] all the Yadava widows became Satis. The *Visnu Purana* says that eight queens of Krishna including Rukmini committed Sati.[15] The *Vayu Purana* has only one instance of Sati. The text is not explicit whether she did actually ascend the pyre.[16] The *Brahma Purana* and the *Harivamsa* fill up the blank. They say that King Bahu's wife ascended the funeral pyre evidently to immolate herself and the sage Aurva dissuaded her from the act. The *Visnu* and *Brahannaradiya* say so explicitly.[17]

The ground on which Aurva appears to have dissuaded the wife of Bahu from her act of self-immolation suggests that the custom was not still regarded with approval. The instance then falls in time and spirit with the period anterior to that of the *RgVeda* which reminds us of an ancient custom of the Sati but shows its discontinuance.[18] This leads us to conclude that the Purana had preserved for us a fact which might be considered historical as it synchronises with the political history of King Sagara.[19] The *Bhagavata Purana* makes explicit mention of Gandhari's burning herself on the death of her husband dhrtarastra.[20] *Agni Purana* considers Sati as an option. It does not recommend it but allows it as a second alternative.[21] The vast majority of the widows that figure in Puranas survive their husbands.

The custom began to become gradually popular from 400 A.D. Bhasa differs from the *Mahabharat* and holds that uttara, Dussala and Pauravi died on the funeral pyres of their husbands, Abhimanyu, Jayadratha and Duryodhana respectively.[22]

Kalidas in the *Kumara Sambhavam* has described how Rati prepares herself for *anugamana* after Kamdeo is killed by Siva. Rati says that she is coming to heaven to meet her husband. In fact she might have gone with him but for the fact that she was unconscious out of grief.[23] She further says, "I am reaching the heaven after burning myself before the heavenly damsels attract you."[24] She requests Basant, the friend of her husband to light the pyre so that she can reach her husband.[25]

"Everybody knows that moonlight goes with the moon and lightening goes with the clouds. If inanimate things do like that, I must follow my husband."[26] She wants to smear her breasts with the sacred ashes of her husband and mount the funeral pyre like lying on a bed of new leaves.[27] A heavenly voice, however, dissuaded her to immolate herself and promised that she would again be united with her husband.[28]

"In some Kannada texts the wife is said to be jealous of the apsaras and therefore insistent on dying with her husband."[29] Vatsyayana points out how clever courtesans gain ascendancy over the mind of their lovers by swearing that they would burn themselves on their funeral pyres.[30] Sudraka in his drama[31] *Mrichchhakatikam* has depicted how Dhuta, wife of Charudutta is ready to mount the pyre when her husband is awarded capital punishment on the charge of murdering Vasant-Sena. She does not care even for her 7-year old son. When dissuaded by the friend of her husband on the ground that a Brahman lady should not mount a separate pyre, she flatly says that she did not care for these rules when her beloved is no more.

In the *Gathasaptasati* there is a reference to a woman being decked for anumarana.[32] A passage of the *Harsacharita* gives a beautiful poetic description of *anumarana*. Here is the glory of the moon-lotuses is said to be "laughing like a woman intent on *anumaran* who is decked with ear-ornaments and wears garlands on her head".[33]

The fifth Chapter of the book describes how the mother of Harsa consigns herself to the flames when her husband, King Prabhakarvardhan's case was declared hopeless by his physicians. When Prince Harsa tries to dissuade her from entering the fire Yasomati remarks:

> "I would die while still unwidowed. I cannot endure, like the widowed Rati, to make unavailing lamentations for a burnt husband. Going before, like the dust of your father's feet, to announce his coming to the heavens, I shall be high esteemed of the hero-loving spouses of the gods. Nay, what will the smoke-bannered one burn of me, who am already on fire with the sight of his heart-rending pains? Not to die, but to live at such a time would be unfeeling. Compared with the flame of wifely sorrow whose fuel is imperishable love, fire itself is chilly cold. How suits it to be parsimonious of a life light as a bit of rotten straw, when the life's lord, majestic as Kailasa, is passing away? Even should I live, yet after the mortal sin of sighting the king's deth, the joys, my son, of my son's rule will touch me not. In those that are consumed by grief felicity is ominous, accursed and unavailing. Not in the body, dear son, but in the glory of loyal widows would I abide on earth. Therefore dishonour me no more, I beseech you, beloved son, with opposition to my heart's desire."[34]

It is evident that to burn herself on the funeral pyre of her husband was considered easier than bearing the separation.[35] It was a general belief that even a husband who had committed sins here in this world would attain heaven with the divine power of his Sati wife.[36] But the wife of a sinner was not expected to become sati.[37] The devoted women in general were always ready to sacrifice their lives for their husband's cause.[38] She gave away her ornaments, took a sacred bath, put on all the marks of a lady with her husband living and entered the fire. After the death of her husband, some of the royal officers and the physician entered the fire.

But in the *Kadambari*[39] Bana strongly opposed the system of Sati.

Varahmihira[40] praised women for their courage and chastity which guided them to embrace their deceased husbands and enter their funeral pyres. The *Priyadarsika*[41] of Harsha records that when Vindhyaketu died in the battle, his wife followed him to the funeral pyre. The *Nagananda*[42] of the same author states that Malayvati having heard the news of her husband's death asked her father-in-law to give her the crest-jewel of Jimutavahan the token of her lord, so that placing it on her bosom, she might end her misery by entering the fire.

In the *Dasakumarcharita,* queen Vasumati was determined to follow her beloved to death. Dandin feels that it was a woman's sacred duty to follow her husband into the world of the dead, whether he was good or mischievous and, therefore, Arthapala's mother had no alternative but to mount the funeral pyre.[43] Hence she wore the prescribed garments, had farewell to her friends, worshipped domestic deities, consoled the lamenting servants and mounted the funeral pyre.

Dandi in his *Dasakumarcharitam* has mentioned the preparation of Sati by Vasumati, the queen of Magadh after the defeat of her husband and his disappearance.

When her Ministers reported that the army had been destroyed and the King (Rajahamsa) was traceless, the queen decided to follow him through *anugamana.*[44] But the Purohita and ministers dissuaded her from this course on the grounds that it was not certain that the King was dead and that she was pregnant and her son was destined to become a Chakravartin after defeating his enemies. Though she kept silent at this, but at night she attempted to commit suicide. But there her husband was unconscious on a chariot and hearing her voice he became conscious.[45]

In *Daskumaracarita* Dandin mentions the case of Arbhapala's mother who proposes herself for committing sati:[46]

> " .... "स्त्रीधर्मश्चेष यददुष्टस्य दुष्टस्य वा भर्तुर्गतिर्गन्तव्याति। तदहमुमुनैव सह चिताग्निाराक्ष्यामि। युवतिजनानुकूलः पश्चिमो विधिरनुज्ञाव्यः" इति।

Arthapala suggests to Burnabhadra that he should advise his (Arthapala's) mother to request the King to grant her permission to accompany her husband in death. "It is the duty of a women to follow her husband irrespective of the fact whether he is good or bad. Hence I will commit Sati. Please permit me to do it."

Accordingly Arthapala's mother Kantimati requested the King Simhaghosha to ailow her to accompany her husband in death after his execution. Arthapala narrates:[47]

> "आनीतश्च पिता मे विविक्तायां भूमो दर्भशायुयाम स्थितोभूत। अथ मदम्बा मरणमण्डनमनुष्ठाय सकेस्णा सखीरामन्त्रय, मुहुरभिप्रजभ मूहुरभिप्रजभ्य भवनदेवमा यत्ननिवारित-परिजाक्रन्तिा पितुर्मे शयनस्थानमेकाकिनो प्राविक्षत्।"

Then my father was brought and he was made to lie down on a bed of Kusa grass. Then my mother, adorned like a Sati ready to enter the pyre came there crying and talking with her friends and offered prayers to family deities and requested the servants not to weepand entered the place where my father was lying.

Earlier she requested the King:[48]

> "एष मे पतिस्तवापकर्त्ता न वेति देवमेव जानाति। न मेहन्स्थास्ति चिन्तायययाफलम्। अस्य तु पाणिग्राहकस्य गतिमननुप्रपद्यमाना भवत्कुलं कलडकयेयम्। अतोऽ. नुमन्तुमर्हसि भर्त्ता सह चिताधिरोहणायय माम्" इति। श्रुत्वा चेत्कर्त्रीतियुक्तः समादिक्षत्क्षितीश्वरः -' क्रियतां कुलोचितः संस्कारः। उत्सवोत्तरं च पश्चिमं विधिसंस्कारमनुभवतुमे भागिनिपतिः इति।

Kantimati said—I do not know if my husband has done you any wrong or not, only God knows. I do not ponder over it. If I do not follow him, it will be a disgrace to my family. Hence allow me to mount the pyre of my husband. The King happily announced—"His funeral rites should be performed according to family traditions. Let my brother-in-law have a pompous funeral."

In Magha's *Sisupalavadha*,[49] we find that when Sisupala's army is ready to march, wives of warriors are prepared to follow them on the funeral pyre in *anumarana*.[50] Finding the Kings (warriors) ready to march for the battle, their wives are determined to perform *anumarana*. The maid servants are weeping, but the ladies are not afraid of the fire. A heavenly damsel wanted to embrace a dead warrior and went to a grove at Sumeru until his wife unable to bear the separation committed Sati and reached the heaven to join the dead warrior.[51] A ready immediatley died after seeing her dead husband and reached heaven almost together so that no heavenly damsel could embrace him.[52]

In the *Venisamhara*[53] we find the mother of a dead hero coming on the battle field to enter his funeral pyre along with her daughter-in-law.

We have a peculiar instance of Sati in Nepal where a mother committed Sati on the death of her son. Visujitamalla King of Nepal (Nepal Samvat 878), was killed by some people. This infuriated the Queen-mother so much that she openly scolded and field on her subjects for their utter silence on her son's tragic death and burnt herself on his pyre.[54] Further we have a unique instance of two sisters committing suicide on the death of their brother, along with the latter's wife.

On the death of Mahendramalla of Nepal in Samvat 694, his sisters Bhavani and Santa along with the former's two wives practised *Sahagamana*.[55]

We have some such instances from *Rajatarangini* of Kalhan. The practice was quite popular in Kashmir and we have numerous references to Sati in *Kathasaritsagar*[56] also. Both the books were written in medieval Kashmir.

In the *Kathasaritsagar* we find many instances of self-immolation. In the story of Birbar brahman, his son was sacrificed for the protection of the king. Out of grief his daughter also died. Then the mother of the children (wife of Birbar) mounted the funeral pyre of her children.[57] Even a prostitute, Kamudika mounted the funeral pyre of king Vikram Singh, though her relatives and friends dissuaded her from doing so.[58] The King had only feigned death to test the prostitute. In the same story, hearing the rumour of the death of King Vikram Singh, his queen Sasilekha entered the fire, as was the practice in Anumarana.[59] In the story of *Chandrasri* and *Silhara,* even a woman of loose character committed Sati[60] at the funeral pyre of her husband. In the story of *Monarathprabha,* she wants to commit sati after the death of Rasmiman.[61]

When King Yasaskar died in 948 A.D., his queen Trailokyadevi became a Sati and followed her husband, just as the Sun is followed by his own light.[62]

Again when Tunga and his son were killed, his daughter-in-law, Bimba entered the fire as a Sati.[63] When King Anantadeo died in 1081 A.D., his queen Suryamati leapt with a bright smile from the litter into the flaming fire. Gangadhar, *Takkibudha,* and the litter carrier *Dandaka* and maid servants *Udda,* Nonika and *Valga,* followed her.[64] Earlier when king Anantdeo had sacrificed his life as if in atonement for his breach of courtesy, his wife in gratitude became the guardian of his interests. To all followers from Prince to Chandala, she gave the daily allowance due to them, just as if she were at ease, in order to fulfil her husband's obligations. Then she made all followers take before *Vijaysa* (Shivalinga) an oath by sacred libation in order to assure the safety of her grandson. When her grandson crying touched her feet with his head, as she handed him the sacred libation, she kissed him on the head, and told him not to trust his father. Then the stood up, and as a Sati herself taking the sword, performed the office of doorkeeper for her husband while she had him adorned for the last rites. She first ordered a hundred mounted soldiers to watch there over her grandson, then she sent forth her husband placed on a litter. Having thus passed one night and half a day, this devoted wife paid her reverence to *Vijayesa* and proceeded outside seated in a litter. When the people saw these two going forth, the horizon was rent, as it were, by their tumultuous lamentations, which mixed with the vibrating sounds of the funeral music. After inspecting the guard of honour by the troops, the queen reached the cremation ground as the day was sinking. Asking for water from the *Vitasta*, she recited the following *sloka* "Those who die with *Vitasta* water in their body, obtain for certain final deliverence, just like those who proclaim sacred learning." When she had drunk the water brought to her, she thus cursed those who had destroyed affection between parents and the son by their calumnies: "May those who have caused the fatal enmity between us two and our son quickly be destroyed together with their descendants." Through this unfailing course of the afflicted queen, Jayananda, Jinduraja and others found an early death. In order to put a stop to the slanderous rumours regarding Haladhar's position as her confidant, the Sati took an oath in proper form, pledging her happiness in a future life. Then she jumped in to the funeral pyre followed by her male and female servants.[65]

When Kshemagupta died in 958 A.D., a peculiar situation was created. While the King was alive, queen Didda had been in enmity with Phalgun, the Prime Minister, on account of her co-wives Chandralekha, who was the daughter of the Prime Minister. Hence out of malice, Phalguna gave a quick assent when on her husband's death she wished to become Sati, seeing other wives of the King ready to immolate themselves. But in front of the funeral pyre, she felt regret, and the minister, Naravahan, moved to compassion prevented her from becoming Sati.[66] When King Tunjin died after ruling Kashmir for 36 years, the queen Vakpusta freed herself from the fever caused by the separation in the flames of the pyre which, to her, were like a bed cover formed of lotus fibres.[67] Kalhan boldly compares with them the flames of the pyre on which the queen became a Sati. The place where this lady followed her husband into death, is known to the people by the name of Vakpustatavi.[68]

When Torman died, his wife wanted to follow her, but her son Pravarasena consoled her and dissuaded her from committing Sati. They instead, went on a pilgrimage.[69] When King Sankarvarma died in 902 A.D., he entrusted the protection of his son Gopalvarma (who was a child then) to his queen Sugandha. Then three queens including Surendra Vati followed the King to death. A clever and grateful Vetavitta (a favourite official of the King) named Jayasimha and two servants, Lada and Vajrasara also followed him. Thus the King's mortal remains were quickly consumed by the fire, together with these six people who had ascended the funeral pyre.[70]

When King Kalash died in 1089 A.D., Mammanika and six other wedded queens, as well as a concubine named Jayamati followed him into death.[71] But the whole of the womankind was disgraced by his favourite concubine Kayya. If she did not remember that her lord had given her the foremost position in his seraglio, no matter, let her not remember it, because she was of low orgin. "But it causes us pain," writes Kalhana, "that she, subsequently residing near *Vijayaksetra,* became the concubine of a village official. Her body, which a King had enjoyed, and which continued comforts had beautified, she yielded to a villager. Shame upon women of lowly mind!"[72]

When King *Utkarsha* committed suicide, his concubine, *Sahaja,* acted honourably. As he had no arms, he applied a pair of scissors to his throat, and cut the vital arteries. As the scissors fell on the ground with a thud, Sahaja became alarmed and saw the blood oozing forth behind the curtain. The noble conduct which she then displayed makes women who are beloved by their husbands carry their heads higher even to this day. While their origin, social position and their love for their respective lords were alike, the conduct of *Kayya* and *Sahaja* deserved blame and praise respectively. She, too, had been a dancing girl attached to a temple (Devadasi). King *Utkarsa* had seen her on the dancing stage, and had taken her as a concubine into the royal seraglio. She made her love shine forth brilliantly, just like gold, by entering the pyre by smearing thickly over her limbs the blood of her lover, which resembled liquified red chalk.[73] Also some other ladies of his seraglio, who had been on the Lohar hill, followed his footsteps by the path of fire.[74] When Chandraraja, the commander of King Harsha was killed, his mother, Gajja committed Sati.[75]

King Harsha in his hatred of the family of Malla had Vyaddamangala, the son of Srilekha's nephew, killed. His wife (wife of the deceased), who was a daughter of the maternal uncle of Malla's sons, and her mother-in-law set their house on fire and burned themselves.[76] After the death of Mallaraja at the hands of King Harsha, his princely consort Kumudlekha and his wife's sister Vallabha, immolated themselves in a fire kindled in their residence. Asamati and Sahaja, Malla's daughters-in-law, who were the wives of Salhana and Ralhana, and daughters of Raja and Avakalya respectively, also burned themselves. Also six female attendants of the ladies of his household died on the same pyre.[77] This happened on the left bank of the *Vitasta,* the water of which became hot by the conflagration of the great house and by the tears hot with grief. Nanda, the mother of future Kings, was in her own seraglio on the other side of the river and was eagerly looking from a high terrace towards the camps of her sons. This virtuous lady burned herself in her house together with her nurse, Candri, who felt unable to see the water which was to be offered at the funeral libations of her whom she had brought up as a child with her own milk. Nanda had not yet seated herself in the flaming fire, but was already surrounded by the flames which were playing around, as if they were her female companions, when she uttered the following curse against the king: "May you, O Sons, before many days do to the family of your father's enemy what the son of Jamadagni did.[78]

There is a reference to an incident which may be likened to the later day *Jauhar* in Rajputana. When king Harsha was attacked and his palace was set on fire, Vasentlekha and other queens, daughters-in-law of the King and princesses of the palace immolated themselves to escape their capture by the *Damars*. Thus seventeen ladies died in the fire.[79]

After the death of King Unhchala, the cunning queen Jayamati, who was eager to live, gave her treasure to Garga (the Prime Minister) in order to raise compassion in him and told him: "Brother, make an arrangement with me." He, however, in his honest nature, took these words to be purely conventional, and prepared her funeral pyre.[80] Kalhana has expressed his strong condemnation against such women. He says that "nobody can understand these women of unscrutable mind, in whose heart there is found, as it were, combined the waviness of their ample locks, the excessive unsteadiness of their eyes and the firmness of their round breasts. Though given to unfaithfulness and killing their husbands, yet they step with ease into the fire. In no manner can one be sure of women."[81] There is a Hindi saying similar to this idea.[82]

While Jayamati, proceeding in a litter, was delaying on the way, Bijjata got in front of her and entered the pyre. As Jayamati was ascending the pyre her limbs were hurt by the pilferers who robbed her in eager desire of her ornaments. When the people saw the two queens being consumed by the flames together with their chowries and parasols, they too, raised lamentations.[83]

King Salhana got Dilhabhattara poisoned. Thereupon his sister who had reviled him (Dilhabattara) for his want of manliness, followed the fitting course of a proud woman by entering the fire.[84] Kalhana has referred to a case where four maid servants and a cook entered the funeral pyre of the chief queen (Meghamanjari) of King Sussala.[85] After the death of King Sussala, four queens came forth from the palace to follow the king into death. The people benumbed by the fear of a hostile attack and by the sudden hard frost, were not able to conduct them to the distant burning ground. Therefore they burned their bodies in haste near the *Vihara* of *Skandabhavan,* not far from the Palace. Thus four queens—Devakha, Taralalekha, Jajjala and Rajalaksmi—were consumed in the fire.[86] Kalhana has cited a case where Kostaka's wife entered the fire even when her husband was not dead but only in jail. Not heeding the advice of her relatives who said that she might yet get back her husband alive, she entered the fire.[87]

Apart from describing these cases where wives, servants, officials, sisters, mothers etc. entered the pyre to follow the deceased, Kalhana seems to justify the practice of Sati. The concubines, too, were expected to commit Sati and many of them actually did so. Kalhana writes:

> Who is meaner than he who forgets that attachment to the master, the recollection of which makes women enter the pyre?[88]

Kalhana refers to Sati in another context. King Jayapida was very wise and he understood many things. The poet contrasts him with foolish kings and says "what the embrance of the wife who is eager to follow her husband unto death, is to the dead man raised on the funeral pyre; what the drink prepared from the juice of sugarcane is to him who has lost all consciousness in a complete swoon, and what the fragrance of a multitude of garlands is to him whose life has passed away. That is, the natural beauty and greatness of things to the fools is useless."

Amir Khusrau on Sati

In one of his historical mathnawis, the *Nuh Sipahr,* or the Nine Skies, written to celebrate the glories of Qutubuddin Mubarak's reign, Khusrau has devoted a whole section, the Third Sky, to the description and praise of India and the Indians. He likens India to Paradise, and shows that because of its fruits, flowers and climate it is better than any other country. The Indians excel in science and wisdom;

they are the inventors of numerals, the creators of the *Panchatantra,* the great book of worldly wisdom that has been translated into Persian, Turkish, Arabic and Dari; their music surpasses the music of any other country..... Also, "there is a thing of which you cannot deny the reality—the dying of Hindus out of devotion either with sword or with fire, a woman dying willingly for her dead (husband) and a man for an idol or a rich man. This is, no doubt, forbidden in Islam, but behold what a noble thing it is! If the law permitted it, many a blessed one would die eagerly like that......"[90]

In medieval Hindi literature there are references of Satis who mounted the funeral pyres of their dead husbands. Chandverdai in his *Prithviraj Raso* mentions the Sati of Sanyogita, at the death of Prithviraj. For want of space we have avoided to extensively quote from Hindi literature.

Kabir, the mystic poet of medieval India uses the imagery of Sati to highlight devotion. He has referred to--Sati, Warrior and mendicant who sacrifice their lives for an ideal. The complete surrender of ego to God is compared to the sacrifice of Sati.[91] A man of such towering genius and spirituality as Kabir so takes for granted the authenticity of the impulse to Sati that he constantly uses it as an image of surrender of the ego to God.[92] Coomarswamy writes: "Let us...sacrifice."[93]

Notice more particularly the beautiful and very interesting poem of Muhammad Riza Nau'i written in the reign of Akbar upon the 'Suttee' of a Hindu girl whose betrothed was killed on the very day of the marriage. This Musulman poet, to whom the Hindus were 'idolaters', does not relate his story in any spirit of religious intolerance or ethical condescension; he is simply amazed 'that after the death of man, the woman shows forth her marvellous passion'. He does not wonder at the wickedness of men, but at the generosity of women; how different from the modern critic who can see no motive but self-interest behind a social phenomenon.[94]

This Hindu bride refused to be comforted and wished to be burnt on the pyre of her dead betrothed. When Akbar was informed of this, he called the girl before him and offered wealth and protection, but she rejected all his persuasion as well as the counsel of the Brahmanas, and would neither speak nor hear of anything but the fire.

Akbar was forced, though reluctantly, to give his consent to the sacrifice, but sent with her his son Prince Daniyal who continued to dissuade her. Even from amidst the flames, she replied to his remonstrances, 'Do not annoy, do not annoy do not annoy.' 'Ah,' exclaims the poet:

> "Let those whose hearts are ablaze
> with the fire of
> Love learn courage from This
> pure maiden!
> Teach me, O God, the way of Love,
> and enflame my
> Heart with this maiden's Fire."

Thus he prays for himself; and for her:

> "Do thou, O God, exalt the head of that rare hidden virgin, whose purity exceeded that of the Houris, Do thou endear her to the first Kissing of her King, and graciously accept her sacrifice."

Shah Abdul Latif on Sati

In Sindhi, Shah Abdul Latif's *Shahju Risala,* is regarded both as a scripture and the perfect master-piece of literature. Shah Abdul Latif (C. 1680-1748) was a *sufi* who spent most of his life in the village of Bhita, near Haiderabad in Sindh. He is believed to have performed the severest austerities and attained the status of a *Shaikh*. His works show evidence of his having ben a scholar, but since it was felt that poetry such as his could only have been inspired, there is a tradition that he was illiterate. For us, he is among those whose spiritual striving and aesthetic taste drew them towards the people, who took as their raw material stories and anecdotes related by wandering minstrels and gave them an inner meaning which illuminated their outward form with a transcendant beauty. Shah Abdul Latif's *Risalo* is a compendium of such stories. We give one below as on example to illustrate how the mythical and the irrational has been used as a means of expressing the absolute value.

Diachu or Diach, the raja of Girnar, had a married sister, who was childless. A *faquir* prophesied that she would have a child, but when he grew up he would cut off Diachu's head. The child, when born, was put into a box and set afloat on the river. It was picked up by a bard, Charanu, who lived in the territory of Raja Anera'e, and he named him Bijalu. He grew up into a musician with magical power, which neither man nor beast could resist.

About the time Bijalu was found afloat, a daughter was born to Anera'e and the pandits prophesied that she would be the cause of much bloodshed. She, also was put in a box and set afloat. Ultimately, she was rescued by a potter called Ratno, and given the name of Sorathi. Once when Sorathi was grown up, Ratno, who was a friend and servant of Anerae, took two months' leave from him, but returned after four months. At this Anerae became angry, and when Ratno returned , he would not greet or even look at him. Ratno excused himself by saying that he was delayed because he had to arrange his daughter's marriage. Anerae asked Ratno if he would accept him as a husband for his daughter, and when Ratno agreed, Anerae sent a marriage procession with torches and drums. But Ratno lived in Diachu's territory, and when Diachu saw this marriage procession, and was told that Ratno's beautiful daughter Sorathi was to be married to Anerae, he called Ratno and asked him why his own claim to Sorathi's hand had been ignored. Ratno replied that she was not worthy of so great a raja, but Diachu had her seized and taken to Girnar, where he married her. Anerae was incensed and attacked Girnar, but failed to conquer it. He then resorted to a stratagem.

He sent a pot of gold coins to the village of bards where Bijalu lived and announced that the pot would be given as a reward to anyone who brought him Diachu's head. Bijalu himself was away and his wife, a bardess, out of sheer greed took the pot, thereby accepting the obligation on her husband's behalf that the condition imposed by Anerae would be fulfilled.

When Bijalu returned and came to know what his wife had dome, he was deeply shocked, but he felt morally bound to fulfil the awful condition. He took his lyre and staff and set off for Diachu's Court. There he enchanted Diachu with his music to such a degree that ultimately he agreed to let him cut off his head. Bijalu took the head to Anerae who, realizing the danger of having such a wizard in his dominion, banished him. Bijalu returned to his village. Here he found Sorathi about to mount the funeral pyre along with another wife of Diachu. He was so moved that he also mounted the pyre, and his wife, whose greed was the cause of this great tragedy, followed him. In the end, all the persons in the story meet again in heaven.[95]

Even in the mid-18th Century, we find the famous Bengali poets like Bharat Chandra and Ram Prasad referring to Sati.[96]

Even after the legal prohibition of Sati, we find some eminent Indians and even foreign scholars speaking very high of Indian Satis. Their ideal of womanhood, fidelity, courage and devotion have been praised beyond measure. Thus Rabindra Nath Tagore, the poet-seer and Nobel laureate, wrote a poem, "Ma bhai" eulogising the Sati Woman.[97] Rabindra Nath in his homage to Sati writes:

> "Salutations be to those grandmothers of Bengal, who sacrificed their lives. She who nurtured the nation do not forget her even if you be in the heaven. O Aryan Women, protect your beloved sons from troubles and anxieties of the world. You were not aware of it, even in dream that by your self-denied chivalry the famous heroes of the world were

ashamed. As in the night you would put yourself silently in the bedstead of your husband after completion of the domestic works; on the last day of conjugal bliss after retiring from household duties, adorning yourself like a newly wedded wife and taking the *sindura* (Vermillion mark) between the parting of your hair with ease and comfort, You have beautified the death and sanctified it too. You have made the funeral pyre a place of eternal bliss like the bed-stead of a newly wedded couple. By your sacred sacrifice of yourself the flames of Bengal have been purified. Our history is mute and silent but the eternal fire has been preaching your message. We will bow down before the fire which is imperishable, which carried your living memories...which is the emblem of your final union..... Death, how easy, how glowing, and how noble it is.....".[98]

J. Talboys Wheeler[99] has quoted Dubois[100] where the following verses by a poet of peninsular India are supposed to express the feelings of the sin while firing the funeral pile of living parent, and furnish a powerful illustration of the inhumanity of the practice. Strange to say, although the dogma of the metempsychosis finds no expression in the rite itself, it is yet introduced in the verses. Extracts from the song of Pattanatta Pillei, as he performed the funeral rites for his mother:

"1. In what future birth shall I see Her, who for ten months, burdened, bore me; and when she heard the word son, lovingly took me up in her rosy hands and fed me from her golden breast?

2. Shall I kindle the flame to consume Her, who for three hundred days of weariness and longing, morn and evening imploring Siva's grace, was borne down by me a burden?

3. Shall I place Her on the pile and kindle it, - Her who in the cradle, on her bosom, on her shoulder,

caressed me, fanned me, singing soothing lullabies?

4. Shall I put the rice into that mouth, my mother's with which she was won't to call me her honey, nectar, her only wealth, her boy?
5. Shall I heap up rice on the head of Her, and place the firebrand with unflinching hand and steady eye, who softly raised me, pressed her face to mine, and called me oft her son?
6. Sorrow for my mother Kindles the fire, deep within and I too have kindled the fire! see it burns it burns.
7. It burns. It burns to ashes—Alas. the hand which soothed me, and reared me, and led me so tenderly that its touch would not have frightened away the timid bird.
8. Is she ashes now? Hath she come already to thy feet. O Siva ? Hath she, ever more gazing on Thee, rejoicing, forgotten me, her son?
9. She was erewhile. She walked in the way. She was here but Yesterday. Today burned, becomes ashes. Come all, unlamenting, sprinkle milk, All is in Siva's power. "(Translated by the Rev. G.U. Bope)

Ananda K. Coomaraswamy[101] cites several cases of Sati from Indian literature. One of them is as follows:

> "In the early lyrics we read of an earthly bride whom the Brahmans seek to dissuade from the sacrifice; but she answers that since her Lord is dead, the cool waters of the lotus pool and the flames of the funeral pyre are alike to her. Another pleads to share her hero's grave, telling the potter that she had fare her Lord over many a desert plain, and asking him to make the funeral urn large enough for both".

Thus there is ample evidence in literature-- Sanskrit, Tamil, Kannada, Sindhi, Hindi, Bengali, English-- of the occurrence of Sati from the age of *Mahabharata* to the present day. Some poets criticised the rite but most of them eulogised and praised the devotion and sacrifice of the Sati.

REFERENCES

1. "सैरन्धायाः सूतपुत्रेण सह दाहं विशां पतिः"
   - *Mbh*, Virat, 23, 8.
2. ददहशुस्तु ततः कृष्णां सूतपुत्राः समागताः।
   हन्यतां शीघ्रमसती यत्कृते कीचको हतः।।
   अथवा नैव हन्तव्या दह्यतां कामिना सह।
   मृतस्यापि प्रियं कार्यं सूतपुत्रस्य सर्वथा।।
   - Ibid., 23, 4ff.
3. J. Talboys Wheeler, *India of the Vedic Age* (Delhi: Cosmo Publications, 1973), pp. 230-31.
4. Herodotus, IV, 71.
5. James Talboys Wheeler, *Ancient and Hindu India: The Brahmanic Period* (Calcutta: Punthi Pustak, 1961), p. 167.
6. *Mahabharat*, Mausala Parva, 7, 18.
7. *Ibid.*, 7, 73-74.
8. पतिव्रता सम्प्रदीप्तम् प्रविवेश हुताशनम्
   ततश्चिच्राङ्ग्दधरं भर्तारं सान्वपश्यत
   ....ततः स्वर्ग गतः पक्षी भार्यया सह संगतः।।
9. इत्युक्तवा पक्षिणी साध्वो प्रविवेश हुताशनम्।
   प्रविष्टायां हुतवहे जयशब्दो न्यवर्तत।।
   - Brahma Purana, Gautami Mahatma, Chap. XI, 80;
   For details see, *Ibid.*, 75-81.
10. *Ramayana*, Uttar Kanda, 17. 14.
11. A.S. Altekar, *op. cit.*, p. 121.
12. *Ramayana*, VI, 32, 32.
13. A.S. Altekar, *op. cit.*, p. 121.
14. *Padmapurana*, Uttarkanda, Chap. 279.
15. अष्टो महिष्यः कथिता रूक्मिणी प्रमुखास्तु याः
    उपगुह्यय हरेदेह विविशुस्ता हुताशनम।
    - *Visnu Purana, V, 38.2.*
16. Upendra Thakur, *op. cit.*, p. 136.
17. *J.R.A.S.*, 1919, p. 355, fn. 4.
18. *Vedic Index*, Vol. I, p. 488.

19. D.K.R. Patil, *Cultural History from the Vayu Purana*, pp. 155-156.
20. *Bhagavata Purana*, 1.13.57.
21. भत्रग्नियाविशेन्नारी सापि
स्वर्गमवाप्नुयात् ।।
- *Agni Purana*, 221, 23.
22. Bhasa, *Urubhanga* and *Dulaghatotkacha*.
23. परलोकं नवप्रवासिनः प्रतिपत्स्ये पदवोमहं नव।
विधिना जन एवं वचितस्त्वदधीनं खलु देहिनां सुखम् ।।
- *Kumar.*, IV, 10.
24. अहमेत्य पतगडवर्त्मना पुनरडकाश्रणी भवामिते।
चतुरेः सुरकामिनीजनैः प्रिये! यावन्न विलोभयसे दिपि।।
- *Kumar.*, IV, 20.
Cf. Romila Thaper, *op. cit.*, p. 16.
25. तदिदं क्रियतामननारं भवता बन्धुजन प्रयोजनम्।
विधुरां ज्वलनातिसर्जनान्नतु मां प्रापय पत्युरन्तिकम्।
- Ibid., IV, 32; See also IV, 35, 36.
26. शशिना सह याति कोमुदी सह मेधेत तहित्प्रलीयते।
प्रभदाः पतिवर्त्मगा इति प्रतिपन्नं हि विचेतनेरपि।।
- *Ibid.*, IV, 33.
27. अमुनेव कषायितस्तनी सुभगेन प्रियगात्रभस्मना।
नवपल्लव वसंस्तरे यथा रचयिष्यतमि तन्द्रं विभावसो।।
- *Ibid.*, IV, 34.
28. *Ibid.*, IV, 39-45.
29. Romila Thaper, *op. cit.*, p. 16.
30. Vatsyayan, *Kamasutra*, VI, 3, 53.
31. *Mrchakatika*, *Act X*:
। नेपथ्ये कलकलः । पुनर्नेपथ्ये । एसा अज्जवारूदत्तस्य बहुआ अज्जा धूदा पद्रे वसणंचले विलग्गनां दारअं आविखवन्ती वाप्फभीरद-णअणेहिं जणेहिं गिवारिज्जमाणा पज्जलिदे पावए पविसदि।
....
धूता-। सास्त्रम। जाद! मुंचेहि मं, मा विग्ध करेहि । भीआमि अज्जउत्तस्य अम्रंगलाकण्णणदो । इत्युथ्याय, अ चलमाकृष्य, पावकविमुंख परिक्रमति।
........विदुपकः - भोदीए दाव व्रम्हणीए भिण्णत्तणेणं चिदाधिरोहणं पाव उदाहरनी रिसीऔ।
धूता - दरं पावाचरणं, ण उप अज्जउत्तस्य अमंगलाकण्णणं।
32. Hala, *Gathasaptasati*, VIII, 33. Bana, *Harsacharita*, Ucchvas V, Sixth para from the end:

33. "दन्तामलपत्रप्रसाधितकर्णिकासु केसरमालाकल्पित मुण्डमालिकासु अनुर्मतुमिबोध-तासु प्रहसितमुखीषु कुमुदलक्ष्मीषु................"
34. *Harsacharita.*
35. Shri Harsha, *Naishad Charita,* IV, 46.
36. *Ibid.,* XIX, 44.
37. *Ibid.,* IV, 79.
38. *Ibid.,* IX, 70.
39. *Kadambari.*
40. "सुकृतज्ञतयागना गतासूनवगुह्य प्रविशन्ति सप्तजिह्वम्।।"
    - *Brihata Samhita,* 74, 16.
41. *Priyadarsika.*
42. *Nagananda.*
43. Dandin, *Sasakumarcharita.*
44. 'वसुमती तु तेभ्यो निखिलसैन्यक्षतिं राज्ञोऽदृश्यत्वं चाकण्योद्विग्ना शोकासागर-मरना रमणनुगमने मतिं व्यधत्त।
    - *Dasakumar Charitam, 1, 35.*
45. कल्याणि, भूरमणामरणगनिश्चितम्। कि च देवज्ञयकथितो मधितोद्धातारातिः सार्वभौमोऽभिरामो भाविता सुकुमारः कुमारसवदुदरे वसति । तस्मादध तव मरणमनुचितम्' इति भूषितभाषितेत्मात्य पुरीहितैरजुनीयमानया तया क्षणं क्षणहीनयां तूस्णीमस्थायि।
    - *Ibid.,* 1, 26.; See also 1, 37.
46. *Das:* 4th Uchchvas.
47. *Ibid.*
48. *Ibid.*
49. Magha, *Sisupalavadha.*
50. समरोन्मुखे नृपगणेऽपि- तदुनमरणोद्यतैकधीः।
    दीन परिजनकृताश्रुजलो न भटीजनः।
    स्यिरमना विचपत्नमे
    - *Ibid.,* XV, 93.
51. वृत्तं युद्धे शूरमाश्लिष्य काचिद्रन्द्रं तूर्णं मेरुकुजं जगाम्।
    व्यकत्वा नागनौ देहमिति स्म भावतयत्नी
    सद्यस्त्द्वियोशासमर्था।।
    - *Ibid.,* XVIII, 60.
52. व्यक्तप्राणं संयुगे हस्तिनीस्था वीक्ष्य प्रेमणा तत्क्षुणादगतासुः।
    प्राप्याखण्डं देवभूयं सतीत्वादाशिश्लेप स्वव कश्चितपुराघ्न्री।।
    - *Ibid.,* XVIII, 61.
53. "हा अति करूणं वर्तते। एषा वरिमाता समरविनिहलं पुत्रं श्रुत्वा रक्तांशु-कनिरसनया समग्रभूषणया वध्वा सहानुध्रियते।"
    - *Venisamhara,* act IV.

54. Upendra Thakur, *op. cit.*, p. 143, fn. 1.
55. *Vrisotsargavidhi*, Ms. (Durbar Library, Kathmandu). The MS is in Sanskrit but its noting is in Newari language. The relevant extract reads:
" संवत 694 भ्रादपद शुक्ल तृतीया वृहस्पतिवार खकुनु रामशरणो विज्याक दिवस श्री महेन्द्रमल्लसहगामिनो वेमात्री भवानी वैभात्री शान्ना- दूइनी हेरा.
....
- Quoted in Upendra Thakur, *op. cit.*, p. 143.
56. पिता तस्य च बालस्य सतः प वत्माययो।
माता तेन समं पत्या निवेश च हुताशनम्।।
- *Kathasaritsagar, Lambak, VIII, Tarang Vi, 160.*
57. न्यस्तापत्यशवां चक्रे दीपाग्निज्वलितां चिताम्।।
शिवं राज्ञोस्तु' चेत्युक्त्वा साध्वी तस्मिंश्चितानले।
ज्वालाजटात्ये न्यपतच्छीतलहृदलीलया।।
Ibid., Lambak IS, Tarang 3,158,160.
58. साच शोकात्कुमुदिका वार्यमाणपि वान्धवेः।
आगत्य तेनेव समं समारोहच्चित्क्तोपरि।।
- *Kath*. X, 2,31.
59. वैरिभिर्विपयो व्यापपनः शशिलेखा तु लोकतः।
देवी राज्ञो मृषा रूत्वा विपत्तिमं वह्निमाविशत्।।
- *Ibid.*, X, 2,38.
60. आरोहच्च समं तेन पत्या सा तच्छुया चिताम।
स्वजनेवार्य माणापि शीलज्ञैः कृतनिश्चया।।
इत्यं दुरवधादेव स्त्रीचित्तस्य गतिः किल।
अन्यासंड़ग् च कुर्वानी म्रियनो च पतिं विना।।
- *Ibid., X, 2, 65-66.*
61. ततोहं तद्वियोगार्त्ता निन्दनी तनुमात्मनः।
प्रवेस्तुमैच्छनलं गृहीत्वा तत्कलेवरम्।।
- *Ibid.*, X, 2, 65-66.
62. अयरोधयधूमध्यात्सती तं पतिमन्यगात।
एका त्रैलोकयदेव्येव स्वप्रभेव विरोचनम्।।
Rajatarangini, Vi, 107.
63. प्रशान्ते तुमुले बिम्बा चतुर्भिर्दिवसेः सती।
तुंगस्नुषा सुताशाहेः प्रविवेश हुताशम्।।
R.T., VII, 103.
64. एवं विशुद्ध शीलत्वं संप्रकाश्य शुचिस्मिता।
कर्णीरथाददाज्झम्पां ज्वलिते जातवेदसि।।

- *R.T.*, VII, 478.
गङ्गाधरस्टक्कबुद्धो युग्मवाऽश्च दण्डकः।
ताबुद्धा नोनिका वल्गाचेति दास्यस्तदाडवयुः।।
-*R.T.* VII, 481.

65. *Ibid.*, 458-481.
Translation, M.A. Stein (Delhi, Motilal Banarsi Dass, 1961).

66. पत्यो मृते सपत्नीनां दृष्टाऽनुमरणं ततः।
दम्भेनामुमूर्षन्तीमनुमेने स तां द्रुतम्।।
निषेधानुबन्धातु सानुतापां चितान्तिके।
कृपालुर्मरणादेताममात्यो नरवाहनः।।
- *R.T.*, VI, 195-96.

67. The fibres of the stalks of the Waterlily are used as a cooling applicatin, See Kalidas, *Abhijnansakuntalam,* Act V, V, 55, 66 & 71.

68. ....तत्यजे ज्वलनज्वालानलिनप्रच्छदे तया।
- *R.T., V, 226-271.*

69. *Ibid.,* III, 123.

70. तिस्त्रः सुरेन्द्रवत्याया राज्ञयो राजानमन्वयुः।
वेलावित्तः कृतज्ञश्च जयसिंहाह्वयः कृतो।।
द्वौ लाडों वज्रसारश्च तं मृत्यावनुजग्मतुः।
इति षडभिश्चितारूढ़े सहसाकृयताग्निसात्।।
- *Ibid., V, 226-27.*

71. सप्त मम्मनिकामुख्या देव्यः परिणयाहृताः।
अवरूद्धापि जयमत्यभिधाना तमन्मगुः।।
- *Ibid.,* VII, 724.

72. *R.T., VII, 725-28.*

73. कान्तास्त्रगेरिकास्यन्दकृत सान्द्राङगूरागया।
प्रम्णो हेम्न इवोज्जवल्यं प्रविश्याग्निं तयार्पितम्।।
- *Ibid., 859.*

74. - *Ibid.,* VIII, 862.

75. स्वामिकृत्योद्यमस्तुत्य सूतिषु स्त्रीषु पूज्यताम्।
गज्जा तज्जननी स्वस नमस्यनय विशच्चिताम्।।
- *Ibid.*,VII,1380.

76. मातुलस्यात्मजा मल्लापत्येयास्तस्य रोहिनी।
श्वश्वा समं स्ववसतीरादीप्य दहने मृता।।
Ibid., VII, 1568.

77. राज्ञी कुमुदलेखाख्या मल्लस्याला च बल्लया।
गृहेष्जुंहुतां वीतिहोत्रै गात्राणि संभृते।।
राजावकल्ययोः पत्न्यो बाले सल्हण रल्हयोः।
स्नषे मल्लस्यासमती सहजा चाग्नि सादृगते।।
सर्वोपभोगभाग्नियस्तदनाः पुर यापिताम्।
परिवाराड़्ग्ना वह्नो पट्र चात्रैव विपेदरे।।
- *Ibid.*, VII, 1486-88.

78. *Ibid.*, VII, 1489-94.

79. वसनालेखाप्रमुखाः सस्नुषास्तत्र चक्रिरे।
निर्यातरोषाः स्वान्देहात्राज्ञयः सप्तदशाग्निसात्।।
Ibid., VII, 1579.

80. Ibid., VIII, 363-64.

81. चिकुरनिचये यत्कोटिल्यं विलोचनयोश्च या तरलतरता यत्काठिन्यं तथा कुचकुम्भयोः। वसति हृदि तद्यासां पिण्डोभवन्ननुता इमा गहनहृदया विज्ञायनो न केश्चन योषित।।
दौः शील्यमप्याचरन्त्यो घातयन्योऽपि वल्लमान।
हेलया प्रविश नयग्निं न स्त्रीषु प्रत्ययः क्वचिते।।
- *Ibid.*, VIII, 365-66.

82. "तिरिया चरित न जाने कोई। पती मार के सती होई।"

83. *Ibid.*, VIII, 367-69.

84. *R.T.*, VIII, 446-48.

85. *Ibid.*, VIII, 1217-25.

86. *Ibid.*, VIII, 1440-44.

87. *Ibid.*, VIII, 2334-39.

88. *Ibid.*, VIII, 1412.

89. आरूढ़स्य चितां बृतानुगरणोद्योग प्रियालिङ्गनं
पुण्डेक्षुद्रवपानमुल्बणमहामोह प्रलुक्षस्मृतेः।
वीतासोरवतंसमाल्यवलयामोदश्चयादृम्भवेभ्दावानां
सुभगः स्वभावमहिमा निश्चेतसतस्तादृशः।।
- *Ibid.*, IV, 501.

90. *Life and Works of Amir Khusrau* by Dr. Wahid Mirza, Baptist Mission Press, Calcutta, 1935, pp. 182-86.

91. साधु सती और सूरमा इन पटतर कोउ नाहिं।

अगम पंथ को पग धरै, डिगै तो कहाँ समाहिं।।

सत्यकबीर को साखी, ।। बम्बई वेंकटस्वर प्रेस, संवत 1977, पृ0 220

साधु सती और सूरमां, कबहू न फेरे पीठ।
तीनो निकसि जो बाहुरै, ताको मुँह अति दीठ।।

वही पृ0 220

टूटै बरत अकाश सो, कौन कहत है झेल।
साधू सती अरू सूर का, अंनी ऊपर खेल।।

वही पृ0 220

कबीर यहु घर प्रेम का, खाला का घर नाहिं।
सीस उतारै हाथ करि, सो पसै घर माहिं।।
कबीर निज घर प्रेम का, मारग अगम अगाध।
सीस-उतारि पगतलि धरे, तब निकटि प्रेम का स्वाद।।

कबीरग्रन्थावली सम्पा0 श्यामसुन्दर दास।
काशी नागरी प्रचारिणी सभा, काशी, 1928

पृ0 69

अब तो ऐसी है पड़ी, मनकारू चित कोन्ह।
मरने कहा डारइये, हाथि स्यंधौरा लीन्ह।।
जिस मरनेथे जग डरै, सो मेरे आनन्द।
कब मरिहूँ कब देखिहूँ , पूरण परमानन्द।।

वही पृ0 69

ही तोही पूछौं सखी, जीवत क्यों न मराई।
मुंचा पीछे सत करै, जीवत क्यूँ न कराई।।

वही पृ0 71

सती को कौन सिखावता है,
संग स्वामी के तन जारना जी।
प्रेम को कौन सिखावता है,
त्याग माहि भोग पावना जी।।

हजारी प्रसाद द्विवेदी, *कबीर*
।। नयी दिल्ली, राजकमल प्रकाशन, 1985।।
तीसरा संस्करण, पेज, 226

92. Anand K. Commaraswamy, *The Dance of Shiva,* op. cit., p. 113.
93. *Ibid.*, pp. 114-15.
94. Ananda K. Commarswamy:

"A man of such towering genius and spirituality as Kabir so takes for granted the authenticity of the impulse to Sati that he constantly uses it as an image of surrender of the ego to God; and indeed in all Indian mystical literature the love relation of woman to man is taken unhesitatingly as an immediate reflection of spiritual experience. This is most conspicuous in all the Radha-Krishna literature."

- *The Dance of Shiva*, p. 113.

95. H.T. Sorely, *Shah Abdul Latif of Bhit* (Oxford Univ. Press, 1940), quoted in M. Mujeeb, *The Indian Muslims* (London: George Allen & Unwin Ltd., 1967), pp. 323-24.
96. *Bharat Chandra Granthavali*, Basumati Edn. pp. 17 & 22; *Ram Prasad Granthawali*, Basumati Edn., p. 65.
97. The poem occurs in the *Vivedha Prabandha*, an anthology of Tagore's Verses published in the "Rabindra Rechnabali," the collected works of the master.
98. Translated from Original Bengali, quoted in D.C. Sen's *Brhata-Banga*, Vol. II, by Chinmoy Dutt for Upendra Thakur, op. cit., pp. 183-84.
99. J.T. Wheeler, *India from the Earliest Ages* (Delhi: Cosmo Publications, 1973), pp. 91-92, fn. 23.
100. *Description of the People of India*, Madras, 1862, p. 221, fn.
101. *The Dance of Shiva* (New Delhi: Sagar Publications, 1971), p. 113.

5

Sati in Inscriptions

We have a large number of epigraphic records referring to the practice of *Sati* in ancient and medieval times. The earliest one is in 191 of the Gupta era (510 A.D), i.e., the Eran posthumous inscription of Goparaja wherein it is said that his wife followed him on the pyre after his death in the battle against the Hunas.[1] This is probably the earliest epigraphic reference to the *Sati*. The battle indicated here represents a phase of the struggle between the Guptas and the Hunas in Central India.

We have the Nepal inscriptions of 705 A.D. wherein Rajyavati, queen of Dharmadeva, bids her son Mahadeva to take up the reins of government so that she may follow her husband. The Belataru inscription of the time of Rajendracoladeva records the interesting story of a Sudra woman, Dekabbe, who is said to have burnt herself on hearing the death of her husband, in spite of strong protests and opposition from her parents and relations. When she burnt herself, her parents erected a fine monument to her.[3] The epigraph is important as it is perhaps the first inscription concerning the "self-immolation of a Sudra wife after her husband's death."[4] This Sati has been compared to *Sri, Gauri,* Saci, Sita, Rati and similar other Hindu goddesses.[5]

Majumdar and Altekar write:

"Of Ravi Varman's reign we have quite a number

> of records, ranging from the fifth to the thirty-fifth regnal year, and a damaged stone record in Kavadi in the Sorab taluq of Shimoga district seems to record the Sati performed by his queen on his death".[6]

Inscriptions from the peninsula refer to women becoming Satis when their husbands died in the battles fought between and among Hindu rulers such as the Chalukyas, Yadavas and Hoysalas, in the period from the tenth to the fourteenth centuries A.D. Many of these inscriptions are located in Maharashtra and Karnataka. The peak period of Sati in these areas was pre-Islamic in that Muslim invasions were not the cause. However, when faced by Turkish armies from the end of the thirteenth Century, the earlier ritual would have continued. The other interesting feature is that most of these inscriptions refer either to families of Kshatriya status or those seeking such status. "One oftquoted inscription of the battle against the Ganga ruler and who inspite of the opposition from her parents became a Sati. Her husband held a high military position under Chola control. Her insistence may have been occasioned, among other thing, by the wish to establish status. The custom, it would seem, was prevalent at this time among those who held high administrative and military positions generally associated with Kshatriyas. Therefore it is likely that members of lower castes holding similar positions emulated the style of the Kshatriyas".[7]

This point of view finds support from M.N. Srinivas theory of "Sanskritization". Dr. S. Radhakrishnan[8] also writes: "In the matter of vegetarian food and the non-marriage of widows even the lowest classes imitate the highest with the increase of confusion, instances of Sati also increased".

We have another grant[9] of Saka 1103 (1181 A.D.) to a temple by Sind Mahamandalesvara Racamalla on a request by two Satis—Dailiyakka and Malapaniyakka—both widows of his general Baciraja.

Another inscription[10] of Cedi samvat 919 refers to three

queens who became Satis.

The Temara gate stone inscription[11] of Saka Samvat 1246 (1324 A.D.) speaks of one Manikyadevi as becoming as becoming Sati on the death of her husband, Amana, an executive officer of the glorious Hariscandradeva. The Mistra Deoli Inscription[12] in Jodhpur refers to two queens of a Gohila Rana as having become Satis. We have, besides, numerous references to Sati—records of Saka 1362 and 1365.[13] One of these Sati records was found in a village named Bamhani of the Damoh district (U.P.) and is dated 1365 Samvat.[14] In another village named Salaiya, 5 Kilometres from Bamhani, there are two Sati records, one dated in 1304 A.D. and the other in 1309 A.D., the former erected during the reign of Vaghadeva and the latter in that of Ala-ud-din. One of them (the former) is lying on a hillock and its date roughly corresponds to Monday, the 9th March, 1304.[15] The second is lying in a field.[16] Both the stones are put on the border of a deserted village, Arhaiya Kheda, which is identical with Baliakheta of the Mahoba plates of Parmardi-Deva, V.S. 1230.[17] We have another Sati-record[18] in Patan (District Jubbalpore) of Saka 1361 and another of Saka 1366 at Singorgarh.[19] In his interesting article[20], Walsh shows at length how the memorial stones usually bear the figure of the upraised arm and of the Sun and the Moon on either side and a group of stars.

The literary evidence from the works of Bhasa, Kalidasa, Bana, Sudraka and Kalhana tends to show that the Sati custom was getting gradually popular in the royal families of northern India from 400 to 1000 A.D. It is, however rather strange that only a few epigraphical records of this period should be referring to the actual cases of the Sati. Negative evidence is never conclusive, but "it is only reasonable to expect that the court panegyrists would not have failed to mention the cases of Sati, when they were eulogising the Kings and queens of their royal families. As it is, only a few epigraphs refer to the Sati cases even in Rajputana, which later become a stronghold of the Sati custom. The earliest among these is that of the mother of the Chahamana

King Chandamahasena, who became a Sati in 842 A.D. The next case is that of Sampalladevi, who became a Sati at Ghatiyala in Rajputana in 890 A.D. We have no other recorded cases of Sati in Rajputana records prior to 1000 A.D."[21]

The enthusiastic advocacy of the Sati custom by medieval commentators began to have an appreciable effect on society only after about 1300 A.D. About twenty cases of Sati are referred to by records in Rajputana between the period 1200 and 1600, most of these are of ladies belonging to the royal or Kshatriya families.[22] In Mahakosala, more than 50 Sati stones near Saugar show that widows belonging to the weaver, barber and mason castes were often becoming Sati during 1450-1824 A.D.[23]

The Karnataka inscriptions also throw some interesting light on the state of Sati in that part of the country. We have in them only eleven cases of Sati during the period 1000-1400 A.D. and forty-one cases during 1400-1600 A.D. Most of these Satis belonged to the Nayaka and Gauda castes who formed the main fighting Sect.[24] A.S. Altekar comments that "it is clear that some Jains had also begun to feel that they ought not to lag behind Hindus in the matter. Inscriptions, however, record only very few cases of Brahmana widows bocoming Satis; it is obvious that the lifting of the canonical ban had not yet succeeded in popularising the custom in the priestly order".[25] Further, we have a Mysore inscription referring to a lady as going forth to the fire-pit to die (to become a Sati).[26] A thirteenth Century Tamil inscription contains the passionate outpourings of the heart of a young childless widow, afraid of the woes and ill-treatment in store for her, after the death of her husband, by her near relatives.[27] The unfortunate widow wails: "If she lived after her husband, she would be the slave of her co-wives (who apparently had sons and were, therefore, going to be de facto owners of the family property). Whosoever said that she ought not to die... those, who did not bind her, and throw her into fire, and kill her would get the sin of prostituting their wives." The apprehension of hellish existence after the death of her husband was one of the many potent causes in later times which prompted a widow to end her life.

In the village of Budhpur and Buram (Manbhum district in Bihar) there are several stones referred to as pillars. Some of them are inscribed, but all are more or less sculptured, the general subjects appear to be a man drawing a bow, sometimes on horseback, but more often on foot, showing that the husbands of those in whose memories these pillars stand were warriors slain in battle. Most of them have animals also, sculptured in the topmost compartment.

In the village of Budhpur, there are a few Sati-pillars; two of them were inscribed, but the weather has not left the writing legible, and whatever is spared has been destroyed by the chisel.[28] The district of Manbhum contains numerous monuments of a peculiar sort, but of a much later date which are crude stone carvings, and are placed here and there in front of the temples. Some of these stones have been described as Sati monuments, but are evidently put up as temple-wardens, just as in modern houses similar figures are pointed near the door.[29] All authorities, from Prinsep to Cunningham onwards, have, without exception, considered them to be either Virakal (monuments to warriors killed in battle or in some cases in hunting wild beasts) or Sati memorials. Jayaswal has dated the inscriptions on these monuments from the form of the letters as being 700 A.D. and 1000 A.D.[30]

These Virakal and Sati-monuments are of great interest as they show examples of weapons and accoutrements, the method of doing the hair, and other particulars of different periods and localities, and in some cases they refer to the names of the rulers and states or districts of the times. The inscription on one of these Sati-stones partially reads: *Rajputra Sri Vadadhuga* (Chadadhuga) and may be dated 900-1000 A.D.[31] On one stone there is a kneeling female figure having a number of bracelets on both arms, there are six on the left arm which is better preserved and there are traces of an inscription on the base of this stone. Another stone is broken but has had a footman—only the legs and dhoti remain. There is an inscription on the base of this stone.

Three stones containing the figure of a female in a small panel are Sati-memorials. On two of these we have an inscription. The one reads: *Gharavati Dhruvakasya* (wife of Dhruvaka) and is dated 1000 A.D. The other reads : *Raja-matae Vada dhuch*(?) or the king's mother Vadadhucha and is dated 70 A.D.[32]

The village of Buram (Manbhum) is also rich in such memorial stones. Some of these are Virakal memorials, but Sati-stones have not been referred to, which shows that they were not standing at the time of Mr. Beglar's visit to Buram in 1872[33], who has described all these temples and monuments at length. They are of grey granite and are much worn, and the features of the faces are entirely worn away and belong to the 13-14th Century A.D.[34]

Besides the above stones, a number of small plaques showing a man and a woman together were found during the excavations of 1940-44 on the site of Ahichhatra (650-1100 A.D.[35] The plaques are thin and rectangular, half of them having rounded tops, and all are made form shallow moulds. The male and female figures stand facing, with the left hand of the male and female figures stand facing, with the left hand of the male and the right hand of the female figure crossed at the back and placed on each other's shoulder. The male figure usually stands on the left but in three cases the position is reversed. The Relief is invariably superficial, with no attention to details of ornaments or drapery. The style is crude, showing similarity with the figures on Sati-stones.

The plaques served a votive purpose being used as offerings near Sati-stones at places called Sati-Caura (places where images of Sati are installed and regularly worshipped by people). The couples on the Sati-pillars in Bundelkhand, where they still abound, are known as Sati-Satta, a term which has been adopted to designate figures of this type.[36]

It may be suggested here that people use the term Satta for those heroes or other on whose funeral pyre, their wives burnt themselves. Although this term seems a misnomer, yet it is popular with the simple folk in the area.[37]

The stratigraphical evidence supported by the style shows the figures to belong to the advanced medieval period. In fourteen specimens the woman wears a petticoat (*lanhga*) as was worn by the Rajput women of that age. Out of thirty-seven pieces, thirty-four are assignable to 9th-11th Centuries. One piece shows an earlier style (about the 8th Century).[38]

As a matter of fact, *Virakal* and *sati*-memorial stones are found in may places throughout India. The Sati-memorials in some cases, in addition to the human figures depicted, bear an upraised arm and hand, with the Sun and the moon on either side as being perpetual witnesses to the Sati's offering; in some cases the hand holds a lime-fruit between the thumb and the fore-finger. This is what is alluded to in old inscriptions where women are said to have given arm and hand. In some cases, this symbol of the upraised hand with sun and moon alone appears. In other cases, there is the figure of a snake, indicating the house-hold deity. In still other cases, there is a niche in the monument for a lamp which is known as "Dewali" (Diwati). The earliest example is a pillar at Balod, now in the Nagpur Museum. This stone had served as a memorial of three successive *Satis* and bears three inscriptions. The two later inscriptions are worn off, but the earliest remains. The characters of this inscription, according to Prinsep, belong to the 2nd Century A.D.[39] One at Baro in Malwa is dated by Cunningham[40] as of the 9th or 10th Century. Another at Satanwara is dated Samvat 1016 i.e., 959 A.D.[41] One at Hindorial in the Damoh district of Madhya Pradesh is dated 1056 A.D.[42] and one at Saura in Jubbalpur district, samvat 1355 and Saka 1220, i.e., 1298 A.D.[43] The earliest Sati-stone discovered in Rajputana goes back to 838 A.D., and there are many others which attest to its prevalence only after the later half of the ninth century A.D. The majority of the old stones, however, belong to the 12th or 13th Centuries.[44]

They are very numerous in Karnataka and the Sagour district of Madhya Pradesh. Khimlas, an old town 65 Km from Sagour, contains perhaps the largest number of these stones, 51 of which are inscribed.

Almost all of them are dated, the dates ranging from samvat 1510 (1453 A.D.) to samvat 1880 (1823 A.D.).[45] A peculiarity of the Sati-monuments is that nearly all of them are placed on the western bank either of a stream or of a reservoir with faces towards the east.[46] Perhaps the finest examples of such monuments are memorials of uncertain date of the Mandi Rajas bearing inscriptions, which record the date of each raja's death, and of the number of queens, concubines, and slave-girls who were forcibly burnt on his pyre. "Even more grim than these are the graveyards in which such memorials venerated by the Rajputs stand; each sacred spot termed "the place of great sacrifice" is the haunted ground of legendary love. Among the altars on which have burned the beauteous and the brave, the harpy (Dakini) takes up her abode and stalks forth to places of silence, but to perform stated rites or anniversary offerings of flowers and water to the manes (*Pitradeva*) of the ancestors."[47]

The wife of Dahir, King of Sind, also became a Sati when her husband was defeated and killed by Mahammad-bin-Kasim, the general of the Muslim ruler Hajjaja, in the ninth century A.D.[48]

In Mithila (North Bihar), two queens of Khandvala dynasty are said to have practised Sati on the death of their husbands. The queen of Raja Purushottam Thakur committed Sati. Raghava-Priya, wife of Raja Raghav Singh also burnt herself on the funeral pyre of her husband. There is still a *Sati*-temple (Matha) at the place of her funeral, to the south of Bhauragarhi (the fortress of Bhoura of the Khandvala Kings). There are no images of gods in the temple except two small clay-mounds. There is also a big tanks there known as *Sati-ada* people of the surrounding villages call the goddess as *Sati-mai* (Mother *Sati*), worship her as village-goddess and offer their oblations.[49]

The Sati memorial stones have been recorded and studied in some detail only in recent years. The location, numbers, chronology and the statements both inscriptional and visual, of the herostones and the associated sati-stones have provided new insights into the history of these areas.[50] Some of these areas were subject to raids by Kingdoms in the vicinity, contesting this territory. The Sati-stones generally occur in the same locality as the hero-stones which commemorated death in the course of a heroic act of either defending the village or a herd of cattle or of killing predatory wild animals and so on sometimes the Sati-stone and the hero-stone are on the same slab. The Sati-stone has a standard set of symbols. The sun and the moon indicating eternity, an upright, open, right arm and hand, bent at the elbow and clearly showing bangles intact (a woman's bangles being broken when she is widowed, the bangles being intact would be an indication of her continuing marital status), a lime held in the hand to ward off evil. On occasion a Sati is indicated by a single standing female figure or a couple, where generally the right arm of the woman has the same features as above.

Romila Thapar[51] writes:

> "Sati-stones like hero-stones occur more often, not in fertile agricultural mainlands but in ecologically marginal areas, where local conflicts and skirmishes would be frequent. Possibly in marginal areas, the process of transition from tribe to jati may have required an understanding of the new norms which would have implications for the inheritance and status of women. Tribal chiefs are also memorialized in hero-stones and this was part of the process of Kshatriyaisation, assimilation into the Sanskritic tradition. Doubtless by now, sati would also have played a part in the adoption of a Kshatriya life style."

Inscriptional and archaeological evidence suggests that the greater occurrence of immolation seems to date to the end of the first and the early second millennium A.D. This was a time of new areas being opened up to settlement by caste-based society and encroachments on a larger scale into tribal areas. New castes emerged in this background of a chain economy, some with antecedents in the earlier pre-caste society. In the competition for status various observances of upper caste society became current. Why the immolation of widows was introduced requires explanation. Apart from other things it may relate to a deliberate subordination of women who had earlier had an important role. As a ritual it was the most traumatic in underlining the subordination of women. Or, it could have been a reaction against the many growing socio-religious movements some of which disapproved of caste differentiations and supported the continuing participation of women in social roles whether as wives or widows and which movements were not always regarded with favour by the upper castes. The immolation of widows may have been seen as a method of demarcating status.[52]

D.D. Kosambi writes:

> A remarkable but not unique case of absorption may be seen a mile beyond Malavli, near the village of Devalem (Maharashtra). The mother-goddess in her thicket is (as usual) several lumps of stone, coated with red. but her name is *Sati-ai*. Fifty feet away is the actual *Sati*-monument to an unknown widow of the feudal period who immolated herself on the spot; but that is now called Gopalapora, The shepherd-boys' dancing-post, because of the custom the lads have of dancing there in a group on certain days. The primitive goddess has become identified with the Sati, and the cults of coalesced. A human *Sati* may be forgotten altogether as such, though the monument remains identifiable by the customary (though not obligatory) bent-arm-and-hand with open fingers. If I am not greatly mistaken, two breast-

> like humps on top of a Sati-stone would indicate *Sahagamana:* that the widow immolated herself on the same pyre with her husband's corpse; a single hump would mean that she followed her husband into the next world some days after his cremation, on a separate pyre: *anugamana*. Such memorials exist at Botai, as elsewhere in our villages. She may be regarded as special protectress of the village even though her name be forgotten as usual. This last is to be seen at *Pimploli,* where a coconut is broken before her uncovered *Samadhi* stone every Sunday, and the meat distributed as Sacrament."[53]

Then there are a large number of Sati temples all over the country, especially in Shekhawati region of Rajasthan. The most important temple is located at Jhunjhunu in Rajasthan commemorating a medieval Agarwal Sati. A legend has now been created concerning this Sati (Narayani Devi) whose insignificant memorial has been transformed into a huge marble temple complex sprawling over many acres. Apart from the main shrine to Narayani Devi, daughter of a trader form Hissar, now termed 'Rani', are 12 smaller shrines named, for want of their original names, after various goddesses of the Hindu pantheon.[54] Although some building had started in the earlier decades of the twentieth century, it was in the post-independence period, notable from the fifties on, that the huge temple complex, still undergoing expansion, acquired its present shape. During the same period the annual *mela* (Fair) was started. A Rani Sati Girls' Primary school was started in 1961, near the temple. In 1986 a new section to the temple and a 51 Kg gold Kalash were added. The Rani Sati Garva Sangh is the managing trust of the temple, and its several branches throughout the country and abroad had by 1983 set up no less than 105 Rani Sati temples in different towns and cities.[55] The devotees of this new cult naturally maintain that they are only worshipping a family Sati. But their lavishing crores of rupees for temple building activity on mouldering medieval Sati mounds as well as on cremation sites of fresh victims in the vicinity, no matter of which caste, belies their claims. In the past three decades, it is these temples with their annual melas, booklets, posters, jhankis, cassettes, etc. Which have been pumping a refurbished ideology of Sati and *naridharma* into the area.[56]

The sacred shrine of Sampati Sati[57] is yet another hollowed place of pilgrimage on the banks of the Ganga in Barh (Bihar) which was erected on the cremation site in November 1928, where Sampati Kuar of village Berhana, a few Kilometres away form Barh was forcibly burnt on the funeral pyre of her husband by her relations. They were later prosecuted and punished. But even today the shrine of Sampati contiues to draw large number of people all the year round. People talk in hushed whispers of miracles effected as a result of prayers offered at that shrine.

The Raj Gonds—an aboriginal tribe of Hyderabad—maintain numerous of the ancestors of the Sitagondi branch of the atram clan. "While other clans have usually one *Sati* shrine which contains in addition the pot with the *Chauwar*, here the Rajas' lineage, the Katora's lineage and the Patel's lineage have each a separate shrine, and together the Sati in these three shrines represent all the ancestors of the clan. No one knows whether these shrines, so like the huts erected over tombs, stand on sites where there were once actually the graves or burning-places of prominent clan-members, but this is by no means improbable, considering that round about are many tombs of recently deceased Atram clansmen."[58]

REFERENCES

1. Fleet, *C.I.I.*, Vol. III, p. 93; D.C. Sircar, *Select Inscriptions*, Vol. I, pp. 335-36.

   Verse 4 of the inscription reads:

   कृत्वा व युद सुमहत्प्रकाश
   स्वर्ग्ग गती दिव्य न ।। रे ।। न्द्र कल्पः
   भक्तानुरक्ता च प्रिया च कान्ता
   भार्य्यावलग्नानुगताग्नि राशिम् ।।

2. *Indian Antiquary,* Vol. IX, pp. 163ff.
3. *E.I.,* Vol. VI, p. 213.
4. *Ibid.,* p. 213.
5. Upendra Thakur, *The History of Suicide in India* (Delhi: Munshi Ram Manoharlal, 1963), p. 150.
6. *The Vakataka-Gupta Age* (Delhi: Motilal Banarasidass, 1967), p. 244.
7. Romila Thapar, "In History," *Seminar,* February 1988, p. 16.
8. Radha Krishnan, *Religion and Society,* pp. 13ff.
9. *E.I.,* Vol. XIV, pp. 265-67.
10. *Ibid.,* XX, p. 168.
11. *Ibid.,* X, p. 39.
12. *Ibid.,* XX, p. 58.
13. *E.I.,* XVI, p. 10, fn. 4 & p. 11, fn. 2.
14. *Ibid.,* XVI, p. 10, fn. 4.
15. *Ibid.,* XVI, p. 11, fn. 2.
16. *Ibid.*
17. *Ibid.,* p. 9.
18. *Ibid.,* p. 11, fn. 1.
19. *Ibid.,* p. 11, fn. 2.
20. Walsh, "Virakal and Sati-Memorial Stones at Budhpur and Buram," *JBORS,* Vol. XXIII, p. 430ff.

    (JBORS-Journal of Bihar & Orissa Research Society).
21. A.S. Altekar, *The Position of Women in Hindu Civilization,* (Delhi: Motilal Banarsidass, 3rd ed., 1962), pp. 129-30.
22. Bhandarkar's list, No. 227, 394, 407, 413, 423, 615, 616, 713, 935, 980, 1009 and 1242. See Altekar, p. 130, fn. 2.
23. Hiralal, *Inscriptions from C.P.* p. 53.
24. *Epigraphia Carnatica,* Vol. IV, 2, HG No. 18.
25. A.S. Altekar, *op.cit.,* p. 131.
26. *Epigraphia Carnatica,* Vol. IV, 2 Hg No. 18.
27. *South Indian Epigraphical Reports,* 1907, p. 77;

    Also Altekar, *op. cit.,* p. 137, fn. 1.
28. *JBORS,* XXIII, p. 431.

29. *Ibid.*, p. 433.
30. *Ibid.*, p. 434.
31. For details of the Budhpur Stones, see Walsh's article in the *JBORS*, Vol. XXIII, pp. 436-42.
32. *Ibid.*, p. 439.
33. *ASIR*, VIII, p. 135 (Report of the Archaeological Survey of India).
34. For details, see *JBORS*, pp. 442-43.
35. V.S. Agrawal, "Terracotta figurine of Ahicchatra, District Bareilly, U.P.," in *Ancient India*, No. 4, p. 178.
36. *Ibid.*, Plate LXXB.
37. Upendra Thakur, *op. cit.*, p. 156.
38. For other details, see V.S. Agrawal, *op. cit.*, p. 178.
39. ASIR, Vol. VII, pp. 136-37.
40. *Ibid.*, Vol. X, p. 75.
41. *Ibid.*, Vol. IX, p. 53.
42. *Ibid.*, Vol. VII, p. 94.
43. *Ibid.*, Vol. VII, p. 41.
44. Upendra Thakur, *op. cit.*, p. 157.
45. *ASIR*, Vol. IX, p. 45.
46. *Ibid.*, Vol. IX, p. 41.
47. Crooke, *Popular Religion and Folklore of Northern India*, pp. 155-56.
48. Upendra Thakur, *op. cit.*, p. 158.
49. *Ibid.*, p. 159.
50. See S. Setter and G.D. Sontheimer, *Memorial Stones*, (Dharwad, 1982).
51. Romila Thapar, *op. cit.*, p. 16.
52. *Ibid.*
53. D.D. Kosambi, *Myth & Reality*, op. cit., pp. 87-88.
54. Sudesh Vaid, "Politics of Widow Immolation," *Seminar*, February 1988, p. 21.
55. *Ibid.*, p. 22.
56. *Ibid.*

57. Upendra Thakur, *op. cit.*, p. 155.

58. Christoph Von Furer-Haimendorf, *The Aboriginal Tribes of Hyderabad*, Vol. III, BK 1, p. 291.;

    For other details see "Sati in Hyderabad," *The Proceedings of Indian History Congress*, 1953, Quoted in Upendra Thakur, *op. cit.*, p. 180.

6

Foreign Accounts of Sati

We have already seen the first historical reference to Sati by Keteus' wife. Thus Greek historians were the first to notice it. From the accounts of Strabo, we practised by the Cathaei tribe in the Punjab in the 4th Century B.C.[1] The practice is said to have arisen from the apprehension that wives should desert or poison their husbands.

We are told by Alberuni[2] that the wives of the dead kings were burnt with them.

Ibn Batuta, a 14th Century traveller tells us that on the rumour of Ain-ul-mulk's death, a rebel against Muhammed bin Tughluq, his wife expressed her desire to be burnt like a Hindu widow.[3] He tells us how he fainted to see the unbelievable courage of a dauntless widow, who gleefully embraced the account of Sati in Malwa and says that the custom was highly esteemed but not obligatory. The Smriti rules relating to the property left by their husbands indicate that the African traveller was correct. According to him, under a law made by the Sultans of Delhi, permission had to be obtained before burning a widow.[5]

Friar Jordanus refers to Sati as peculiar custom in the Sind region in the third decade of the 14th Century.[6] Sulaiman writes: "Sometimes when the Corpse of a king is burnt, his wives cast themselves upon the pile and burn themselves, but it is for them to choose whether they will do so or not".[7] Amir Khusrau had conceded that Sati and *jauhar* were "no doubt magical and superstitious, nevertheless they are heroic."[8] Duarte Barbosa, who was in the Indian Ocean in 1508-9 A.D. records: "When the King (of Vijayanagar) dies four or five hundred women burn themselves with him".[9] Fernao Nuniz who visited Vijayanagar during Achyuta's reign (1530-1542 A.D.) writes— "He (Achyuta) has five hundred wives and as many less or more as he wants, with whom he sleeps, all of these burn themselves at his death".[10]

Sati in Vijayanagar Empire

In 1327 the Kingdom of Karnata was attacked by Mahamud Tughluk, the Sultan of Delhi. The Delhi army laid seige to the fortress of Kumata. When Ramanatha found further defence useless he commanded a great fire to be prepared and lighted. Then he burnt his furniture and said to his wives and daughters, 'I am going to die, and such of you as prefer it, do the same'. Then it was seen that each one of these women bathed herself, rubbed her body with sandal wood, kissed the ground before the Rai of Kampila, and threw herself upon the pyre and perished. The wives of his nobles and chief men followed them and other women also did the same.

This instance of *Jauhar* has been described by many authors including P.B. Desai & others. Nicholo-de-Conti (a Venetian traveller, who was in India sometime between 1420 and 1444 A.D.) records that the king of "Bizengalia" (Vijayanagar) takes to himself 12,000 wives of whom 4000 follow him on foot where-ever he may go and are employed in the service of the kitchen. A like number, more handsomely equipped, ride on horse back. The ramainder are carried by men in litters of whom 2,000 or 3,000 are selected as his wives on condition that at his death they should voluntarily burn themselves which is considered to be great honour for them."[11]

Manucci deals extensively with the burning of Brahman and Rajput widows with their husbands and says that sometimes force was used to induce them to commit Sati.

He himself rescued one such widow, who was eventually married to a European friend of his.[12] Manucci describes the scene as follows:

> Wood is heaped up to a height of eight or nine feet, and about the same length and breadth. Upon the top the corpse of the dead Brahman is laid, dressed as when alive, the head to the south and the feet to the north. After he has been laid thus on the bonfire, there comes the wise man of the village and pronounces certain magic words at the five organs of sense, and anoints them with butter. The anointing done, the parents and the nearest relations throw four or five grains of uncooked rice into his mouth.

When these ceremonies are finished they turn the body over on its side. As they do so "the widow without tears—nay, on the contrary, all radiant and joyous mounts to the top of the pyre, and lying down on her side, closely embraces her dead husband. At once the relations bind her feet strongly by two ropes to two posts driven into the ground for the purpose. Next they throw some more wood and dried cowdung on the two bodies, the quantity is almost as much as that beneath them. The woman is then spoken to by her name, and three times distinctly she is called on to say whether she consents to go to heaven. To this she replies in the affirmative. Her answers having been received, they apply a light, and when the bodies have been consumed, each man returns home envying the firmness and constancy which the woman has been granted the felicity of displaying".[13]

Among the caste of Rajahs it is imperative that on the husband's death the wife be burnt alive with his body, for, should regard for her own honour even not force her to this act, the relations will force her to it, it being an inviolate custom of their caste. It is so whether the husband dies at home of disease or of wounds upon the field of battle. The latter death is common among Rajahs, for all who are not princes are soldiers ..... Since it is one of the fundamental rules of their caste never to give way, but either to die or conquer, those with a high sense of honour are usually compelled to die in battle. The only reward they gain by their efforts is the fame not having turned the back on an enemy.... No sooner has news of a Rajah's death arrived in his country, and the wife is satisfied that he no longer lives, than she is accorded three days of grace. During those days she is permitted to adorn herself as magnificently as she can; and thus arrayed she goes about the streets with lemons tied round her head like a crown (as a symbol of good luck). Her body is uncovered from the waist upwards, and rubbed over with saffron, as also is her face. In this state she takes leave of all those she meets in the streets with a smiling face and free manners and speeches repugnant to her sex and her claim to nobility. When the three days have past, they prepare in an open field a circular pit, deep and wide, which is filled with wood and cowdung. Fire is then applied. On beholding this pyre, she who is to be the victim of her honour, issues, clad in new attire, covered with diverse coloured flowers, some arranged like crowns, other like necklaces, escorted by all her friends, male and female, she approaches the fire. Before it stands a small screen about five feet high. Over its top they throw into the fire a little saffron and some butter and other spices. After prayers, the heroine withdraws about forty paces and returns two times, one after the other, to the place she started from, and each time performs the same ceremonial. At length she retires for the third time some forty paces farther than before, at that moment the screen before the fire is withdrawn. Then, with a rush, she bounds into the pit, and in a short time, there is nothing left but her ashes to furnish an epitaph on her constancy. The Hindus think so highly of those who are burnt in this way that they assert their reincarnation as goddesses in the heaven of Vishnu; and in that equally there are erected to them statues as soon as they are dead. This is done equally for the husband. They assume that men blessed with wives of such great virtue as to sacrifice life for their honour, must without fail be placed among the gods.

But if any wife is found to have greater love of life then of honour, her relations do not leave her to enjoy it for very long, for they throw her into the fire by force, where she ends by undergoing the same suffering without acquiring the same laudations. Thus it is much better for them to endure this hard penalty with firmness and equanimity than to be subjected to it by the violence of others.[14]

Manucci has described the funeral scene in great detail. According to him it is wonderful to see what is done when any Hindu Rajah (Rajput) expires. Before he is taken away to the cremation ground, his head and beard are shaved; his whole body is annointed with essence of rose, his body is bound up in fine cloth smeared with jasmine oil mixed with saffron. The body is laid on logs of sandalwood bound together in the shape of an open bier. The women who are to be burnt with him follow; they are women with whom the Rajah had lived. The principal wife, who has sons, is preserved to maintain the family line. "The women sacrificed are commonly fifteen, twenty, or even thirty in number, as I have seen at various times."[15]

It is memorable to see these women on horse back surrounding the corpse, and calling out thousands of praise of their husband, the good life he led, and the pleasure he enjoyed here below. Feeling under an obligation for so many favours received, they look forward in the next life to receive still greater delight in his society there. All this is carried out with much joy and animation, they being richly clad, oiled and perfumed.

Reaching the cremation ground they descend gracefully from their steeds, and assist in lifting the bier on to the heap of wood. This stands in a pit. The principal wife among them places herself on one side, embracing the corpse and uttering innumerable praise; the others range themselves round the body in the same way. The burners set fire to the wood all round, and dexterously empty on it pots of oil and butter to increase the rapidity of the cremation. When the fire has taken they throw on more oil, and when the heat reaches them the women naturally move and begin to shriek. They are soon choked by the smoke, while the men surrounding the pyre raise a great noise with drums and gongs and loud shouts, while the burners skilfully force them to lie down by thrusting at them with poles. Thus are they burnt both for this life and the next.

Next day the Brahmans and many relatives go to the spot and collect the bones, and send them to be thrown into the Ganges, whatever the distance may be. Some people send them to be thrown in the river at the Tirtha *Sangam* at Allahabad.

If such princes die in battle, the women immolate themselves with still greater alacrity on receiving the turban sent them as a sign of their husbands' death. With it in their hands they are cremated. "I have seen some die with their husband's body in their arms without making a sign of movement. The reason is that the Brahmans provide them with certain *beverages bhang* (hemp), opium, and such like, which entirely stupefy them."[16]

Others, by use of sorcery, become eager, ardent, made demanding that the authorities put no hindrance in their way when in search of their beloved alleging as a reason that they are suffering acutely from deprivation of their loved one.

Manucci cites a case in this connection. At Vizagapalao (Visakhapattana) Mestre Olca (Mr. Holcombe)[17] refused permission for the burning of a woman. She appeared before him, and with great anxiety prayed that no impediment be set against her desire. Mr. Holcombe and others present marked that she seemed to have abandoned her feminine nature. He persuaded her in the name of humanity not to burn herself. He even undertook to support her for the rest of her life. This talk caused her pain, and she persisted in demanding his permission. Then Mr. Holcombe spoke secretly to a Brahman who was with her, promising him a sum of money if he removed the apprehensions that possessed the woman. If he did not effect this, he warned him, he, too, would have to burn with her. He, then, sent orders to close the factory gates as if quite ready to act. The Brahmans, out of greed and fear, went behind the woman without her being aware of it, and gently touched her clothes at the back with their fingers. She totally changed colour, and, raising her hands to her face, and drooping her head in a shamefaced way, went back to her house.[18] Sati did not even leave some Muslim observers unimpressed, as is clear from the "poem of Muhammad Riza Nau'i, written in the reign of Akbar upon the 'suttee' of a Hindu girl whose betrothed was killed on the very day of the marriage.[19]

"The Hindu bride refused to be comforted and wished to be burnt on the pyre of her dead betrothed. When Akbar was informed of this, he called the girl before him and offered wealth and protection, but she rejected all his persuasion as well as the counsel of the Brahmans, and would neither speak nor hear of anything but the Fire.

Akbar was forced, though reluctantly, to give his consent to the sacrifice, but sent with her his son Prince Daniyal who continued to dissuade her. Even from amidst the flames, she replied to his remonstrances, Do not annoy, Do not annoy, Donot annoy'. 'Ah', exclaims the poet:

> Let those whose hearts are ablaze with the Fire of Love learn courage from this pure maiden;
>
> Teach me, O God, the Way of Love, and enflame my heart with this maiden's Fire.

Thus he prays for himself, and for her:

> Do Thou, O God, exact the head of that rare hidden virgin, whose purity exceeded that of the Houris,
>
> Do Thou endear her to the first kissing of her king, and graciously accept her Sacrifice?

Nicoli Conti informs us that financial pressure was often exercised, the widow being informed that she would lose her fight to *Stridhans,* if she decided to survive.[21]

Francois Bernier, the French physician at the court of Aurangzeb, witnessed a Sati while journeying from Ahmedabad to Agra at which "five slaves... were so moved with pity and tenderness towards this mistress" who was committing Sati that they burned with her. Bernier, however, was not moved or rather, was moved to indignation.[22] He has narrated the pathetic case of a child widow of 12 being burnt against her will at Lahore.[23] Bernier, while describing a case of which he was an eye witness, states that it is impossible to describe the brutish boldness or the ferocious gaity depicted on the woman's countenance; her step was undaunted, her conversation was free from all perturbation, her easy air was free form all dejection, her lofty courage was void of all embarrassment. She took a torch and with her own hand she lighted the fire. It appeared to be a dream, but it was stern reality.[24]

J.B.Tavernier, a 17th Century traveller narrates how a widow of twenty-two at Patna held her hand in the flame of a torch till it burnt to cinders in order to convince the officer that she was a willing party and was not afraid of fire.[25] But he also comments with a touch of irony, "the idolators do not only burn the bodies of their dead, but the bodies of the living. They scruple to kill a serpent, or a louse, but account it a meritorious thing to burn a living wife with the body of the deceased husband".[26]

Thomas Herber, an Englishman published his accounts of *Travels in Africa and Asia the Great* in 1638. He witnessed a Sati at Nagapatan on the Coromandel coast. He gives a touching account thereof and then brings it to a poetic conclusion.[27] The Jesuit missionary, de Nobili, also witnessed such scenes in the 17th Century. He was impressed "by the ecstatic devotion with which many of these young widows went to their deaths. The Spirit in which they did so he found admirable though he felt it could have been expended in a much better cause".[28]

The *Akbarnama* informs us:

"In the interior of Hindustan it was the custom, when

> a husband died, for his widow willingly and cheerfully to cast herself into the flames (of his funeral pile) although she may not have lived happily with him. Occasionally love of life holds her back, and then the husband's relations assemble, light the pile, and preserve honour and character of the family (by burning the widow). But since the country had come under the rule his gracious Majesty (Akbar), inspectors had been appointed in every city and district, who were to watch carefully over these two cases, to discriminate between them, and to prevent any woman being forcible burnt."[29]

The book also cites a case in which Akbar intervened personally.

"JaiMal (son of MalDeo) who had been sent with his forces to join the amirs in Bengal, died of sunstroke in the Vicinity of Chausa. His wife, the daughter of Muna Raja (Mota Raja(?) vide Ishwari Prasad, *Muslim Rule in India,* p. 84) was unwilling to burn but her son Udi Singh with a party of his bigoted friends, resolved upon the sacrifice. The matter came to the Emperor's knowledge, and his feeling of justice and humanity made him fear that if he sent messagers to stop the proceedings, some delay might occur. So he mounted his horse, and rode with all speed to the place. As the facts were not fully known, some of these men, in their thoughtlessness, were disposed to resist and make disturbances. But when His Majesty arrived, Jagganath and Rai Sal came forward to meet him, and brought the leader of those foolish men to him. He accepted their assurance of repentance, and only placed them in confinement."[30]

Jahangir[31] in his Memoirs refers to this practice. The people of Rajour (near Kashmir) were Muslims at the time of Jehangir. It is said they were previously Hindus whom Sultan Firuz had converted to Islam. But they were still called Rajas. They still had "the marks of the time of ignorance. One of those is that just as some Hindu women burn themselves along with their husbands' bodies, so these women are put into the grave along with their dead husbands. I heard that recently they put alive into the grave a girl of ten or twelve along with her husband who was also of the same age."

Jehangir condemned this practice among the local Muslims and issued a decree that "hereafter they should not do such things, and whoever was guilty of them, should be capitally punished."[32]

Pietro della Valle was impressed by the courage of the average Sati. "If I knew (of a lady about to become a Sati), I will not fail to go and see her and honour by my presence her funeral with that compassionate affection, which such a great conjugal fidelity and love seem to deserve."[33] Mustaqui has recorded the case of a betrothed but still unmarried women who insisted on committing Sati. The betrothed husband died in trying to save his sweetheart from a serpent, which eventually bit him with fatal effects. Though not yet married, the girl insisted on becoming a sati and burnt herself on the funeral pyre of her lover.[34]

Abbe J.A. Dubois in his book has dealt with this issue. He has given accounts of Satis he witnessed and has expressed his horror over the practice. He also suggests some measures to prohibit it. The book was originally written in French before the ban of Sati in 1829.

According to him, although the ancient and barbarous custom which imposes the duty on widows of sacrificing themselves voluntarily on the funeral pyre of their husbands has not been expressly abolished, it is much more rare nowadays than formerly, especially in the southern parts of the peninsula. "In the north of India and in the provinces bordering on the Ganges, however, women are only too frequently seen offering themselves as victims of this horrid superstition, and either through motives of vanity or through a spirit of blind enthusiasm, giving themselves upto a death which is as cruel as it is foolish."[36]

He reports that Muslim rulers prohibited the Sati without

free consent of the widow, but the 'Wretched fanatics' have been successful in 'bribing' subordinate officials for getting the required permission.

He further writes that it is principally in the noble caste of Rajahs that the Suttee originated. "It was looked upon as a highly honourable proof of wifely attachment and love which enhanced the glory of the families of these wretched victims of blind zeal. Should a widow, by reason of a natural fondness for life or through lack of courage, endeavour to avoid the honour of being burnt alive on the funeral pyre of her deceased husband, she was considered to be offering a gross insult to his memory."[37]

Dubois holds that widows did not always exercise "their own free will and resolution," though he cites a case where the widow refused to become a Sati. The Prince of Cangoondy in Karnataka died. But "neither entreaties nor threats were spared to induce his widow to allow herself to be burnt alive with him. It was urged that this honourable custom had been observed for a long time past in the family, and that it would be a great pity, indeed, to allow it to fall into disuse. The funeral ceremonies were delayed from day to day in the hope that the widow would at last make up her mind to prefer a glorious death to a remnant of life spent in contempt and approbrium. It was a fruitless attempt! The obstinate princess turned a deaf ear to all the pressing entreaties of her relatives; and ultimately the deceased was obliged to depart alone to the other world."[38]

It must, however, be confessed that "some widows committed this folly readily enough, spurred on as they are by the thought of the wretchedness of widowhood, by vanity, by the hope of acquiring notoriety (fame?), perhaps also a genuine feeling of enthusiasm. It should be remembered that they are awarded boundless honours, and are even deified after death. Vows are made and prayers addressed to them, and their intercession in sought in times of sickness and adversity. Such remnants of their bodies as have not been entirely consumed by the fire are most devoutly gathered together, and on the spot, where they have sacrificed themselves, small mounumental pyramids are erected to transmit to posterity the memory of these brave victims of conjugal affection—a tribute all the more conspicuous, because the erection of tombs is almost unknown among the Hindus. (In some old Hindu houses, even to this day, may be seen, impressed with turmeric paste on the walls, the marks of the hands of women who underwent Suttee). In a word, women who have had the courage to deliver themselves so heroically to the flames are numbered among the divinities, and crowds of devotees may be seen coming in from all sides to offer them sacrifices and invoke their protection."[39]

To these inducements of vain and empty glory—sufficient of themselves to make a deep impression on a feeble mind—must be added the entreaties of relatives, who, if they perceive the slightest inclination on the part of the widow to offer up her life, spare no means in order to convince her and force her to a final determination. At times they go so far as to administer drugs, which so far deprive her of her senses that under their influence she yields to their wishes. This inhuman and abominable method of wheedling a consent out of the unhappy woman is in their opinion justified, because her tragic end would bring great honour and glory to the whole of their family.[40]

When a woman, after mature deliberation, has once declared her intention to commit sati, her decision is considered irrevocable. She cannot afterwards retract; and should she refuse to proceed of her own free will to the funeral pyre, she would be dragged to it by force. The Brahmans who regulate all the proceedings of the tragedy, and also her relatives, come by turns to congratulate her on her heroic decision and on the immortal glory which she is about to acquire by such a death—a death which will exalt her to the dignity of the gods. All possible means which fanaticism and superstition can suggest are brought to bear upon her in order to keep up her courage, to exalt her enthusiasm, and to excite her imagination. When, at last, the fatal hour draws nigh, the victim is adorned with rare elegance. She is clothed in her richest apparel, is bedecked with all her jewels, and is thus led to the funeral pyre.

It is impossible for me to describe the finishing scenes of their dreadful ceremony without feelings of distress.[41]

Most Sudras, as well as the Hindus of the Saiva Sect, bury their dead instead of burning them, and there are several instances of wives having been buried alive with their deceased husbands.[42]

Dubois has related two incidents of Sati to illustrate his point. In 1794, in a Village Tanjore district named Pudupettah, a Vaisya of some importance died. His wife, aged about 30 years, announced her intention of committing Sati. The news spread rapidly and a large number of people flocked together from all sides to witness the spectacle. When everything was ready for the ceremony, and the widow had been richly clothed and adorned, the bearers stepped forward to remove the body of the deceased, which was placed in a sort of shrine, ornamented with costly stuffs, garlands of flowers, green foliage, etc., the corpse being seated in it with crossed legs, covered with jewels and clothed in the richest attire, and the mouth filled with betel. Immediately after the funeral car followed the widow, borne in a richly decorated palanquin. On the way to cremation ground she was escorted by an immense crowd of eager sight-seers, lifting their hands, towards her in token of admiration, and rending the air with cries of joy. She was looked upon as already translated to the paradise of Indra, and they seemed to envy her happy lot.

While the funeral procession moved slowly along, the women spectators tried to move closer to her to congratulate her on her good fortune and expecting that, by virtue of the gift of prescience, which such a meritorious attachment must confer on her, she would be pleased to predict the happy things that might befall them here below. With gracious and amiable mien she declared to one that she would long enjoy the favours of fortune; to another, that she would be the mother of numerous children who would prosper in the world; to a third, that she would live long and happily with a husband who would love and cherish her; to a fourth, that her family was destined to attain much honour and dignity; and so forth. Then she distributed among them leaves of betel; and the extraordinary eagerness with which these were received clearly proved that great value was attached to them as relics. Beaming with joy, these women then withdrew, each in the full hope that the promised blessing of wealth and happiness would be showered on her. During the whole procession, which was a very long one, the widow preserved a calm demeanour. Her looks were serene, even smiling. Dubois adds: "Several travellers have said, and I am inclined to believe it, that they force upon these wretched victims of superstition a kind of drink, which confuses the mind and prevents them from forming a correct notion of the dreadful torture to which they are being led. This beverage, they say, consists of a decoction of saffron. It is known that dried saffron pistils (*Crocus Sativus*), taken in large quantities, cause violent and convulsive laughter, sometimes terminating in death."[43]

When, however, the widow reached the fatal place, it was observed that her firmness suddenly gave way. Plunged, as it were in gloomy thought, she seemed to pay no attention whatever to what was passing around her. Her looks became wildly fixed upon the pyre. He face grew deadly pale. Her very limbs were in a convulsive tremour. Her drawn features and haggard face betrayed the fright that had seized her, while a sudden weakening of her senses betokened that she was ready to faint away.

The Brahman, who conducted the ceremony, and her relatives ran quickly to her, trying to keep up her courage and to revive her drooping spirits. All was of no effect. The unfortunate woman bewildered and distracted, turned a deaf ear to all their exhortations and preserved a deep silence.

She was then made to leave the palanquin, and as she

was scarcely able to walk, her people helped her to drag herself to a pond nearby. She plunged into the water with all her clothes and ornaments on, and was immediately afterwards led to the pyre, on which they body of her husband was already laid. The pyre was surrounded by Brahmans, each with a lighted torch in one hand and a bowl of ghee in the other. Her relatives and friends, several of whom were armed with muskets, swords and other weapons, stood closely round in a double line, and seemed to await impatiently the end of this shocking tragedy. This armed force was intended not only to intimidate the unhappy victim in case the terror of her approaching death might induce her to run away, but also to overawe any person who might be moved by a natural feeling of compassion and sympathy; and so tempted to prevent the accomplishment of the homicidal sacrifice.

At last, the Brahman gave the fatal signal. The poor widow was instantly divested of all her jewels and dragged, more dead than alive, to the pyre. There she was obliged, according to custom, to walk three times round the pyre, two of her nearest relatives supporting her by the arms. She accomplished the first round with tottering steps, during the second her strength wholly forshook her, and she fainted away in the arms of her conductors, who were obliged to complete the ceremony by dragging her through the third round. Then at last, senseless and unconscious, she was cast upon the corpse of her husband. At that moment the air resounded with noisy acclamations. The Brahmans, emptying the bowls on the dry wood, applied their torches, and in the twinkling of an eye the whole pyre was ablaze. Three times was the widow called by her name. But alas! She made no answer.[44]

The last King of Tanjore died in 1801, leaving behind him four lawful wives. The Brahmans decided that two of these should commit Sati. It would have been an everlasting shame to them and the grossest insult to the memory of the deceased King had they hesitated to accept this singular honour. Being fully convinced that no means would be spared to induce them to sacrifice themselves either willingly or unwillingly, they made a virtue of necessity and seemed perfectly ready to yield to the terrible lot which awaited them.

At some distance from the royal palace a square pit of no great depth, and about 12 to 15 feet square, was excavated. Within it was erected a pyramid of sandalwood, resting on a kind of scaffolding of the same wood. The posts which supported it were so arranged that they could easily be removed, and thereby cause the whole structure to collapse suddenly. At the four corners of the pit were placed huge brass jars filled with ghee, to be thrown on the wood in order to hasten combustion. The funeral procession was headed by a large force of armed soldiers. Then followed a crowd of musicians, chiefly trumpeteers, who made the air ring with the dismal sound of their instruments. Next came the King's body borne in a splendid open palanquin, accompanied by his *guru* (preceptor), his principal officers, and his nearest relatives, who were all on foot and wore no turbans in token of mourning. Among them was also a large number of Brahmans. Then came the two queens, each borne on a richly decorated palanquin. They were loaded, rather than decked, with jewels. Several ranks of soldiers surrounded them to maintain order and to keep back the great crowds that flocked in from every side. The queens were accompanied by some of their favourite women with whom they occasionally conversed. Then followed relatives of both sexes, to whom the victims had made valuable presents before leaving the palace. A large crowd of Brahmans and people of other castes followed in the rear.

On reaching the spot, the queens were required to perform ablutions and other ceremonies which they did without hesitation and without the least sign of fear. When, however, it came to walking round the pyre, it was observed that their features underwent a sudden change. Their strength seemed to forsake them in spite of their obvious efforts to suppress their natural feelings. During this interval the body of the King had been placed on the top of the pyramid of sandalwood. The two queens, still wearing their rich attire and ornaments, were next compelled to ascend the pyre. Lying down beside the body of the deceased King, one on the right and the other on the left, they joined hands across the corpse. The officiating Brahmans recited in a loud voice several *mantras*, sprinkled the pyre with holy water, and emptied the jars of ghee over the wood, setting fire to it at the same moment. This was done on one side by the nearest relative of the King, on another by his *guru*, on others by leading Brahmans. The flames quickly spread, and the props being removed, the whole structure collapsed. Then all the spectators shouted aloud for joy. The queens' relatives standing around the pyre then called to them several times by name, and it is said that, issuing from amidst the flames, the word Yen (What?) was heard distinctly pronounced. "A ridiculous illusion, no doubt, of minds blinded by fanaticism; for it could never be believed that the unfortunate victims were at that moment in a condition to hear and to speak."[45]

Dubois comments with disgust:

> "It is indeed unaccountable how these Brahmans, who are so scrupulous and attach so much importance to the life of the and indignation at the very sight of a cow being slaughtered can, with such savage cold-bloodedness and wicked satisfaction, look upon so many weak and innocent human beings, incited by hypocritical and barbarous inducements, being led with affected resignation to a punishment so cruel and underserved."[46]

The Travels of Peter Mundy (published by the Hakluyt Society in 1914, Vol. II, p. 34-36), gives an account of the burning of a widow at Surat in 1630 with a sketch which shows the widow having on her lap the head of her deceased husband. The author further says that the practice had become rare in his time as a special license from the Ruler or the Governor had to be obtained under the Mughals.[47]

Barbosa, a Portuguese traveller, also describes the burning of a Sati in the Vijayanagar Kingdom (Vide, trans. by M.L. Dames, Vol. I, pp. 213-14).[48]

H.T. Colebrook, who had spent the best part of his life in Bengal, wrote in 1795, "Happily the martyrs of this superstition have never been numerous. It is certain that the instances of widow's sacrifices are now rare".[49] He wrote a paper describing the procedure of Sati.[50]

Marco Polo, a Venetian traveller of the latter half of the 13th Century visited India. He wrote that widows burnt themselves with their dead husbands and received great praise for so doing.

Ralph Fitch, an English merchant visited in India 1585. He writes, "When the husband dies, his wife is burnt with him; if she refuses, her head is shaved, and she is held in no account."[51]

Edwin Arnold admires such women who commit Sati. He writes:

> "It was a splendid courage and a beautiful faith that inspired these Indian wives. 'Witness that I die, for my Beloved, by his side,' was the farewell of the Sati. It was not very wrong of me, it may be hoped, to lay a flower upon the carved stone which recorded where the Sati had last set her fearless little foot upon this earth of selfish hearts and timid beliefs."[52]

Wheeler[53] has quoted Dubois[54] to express the feelings of a son while firing the funeral pyre of a living parent. It furnishes "a powerful illustration of the inhumanity of the practice. Strange to say, although the dogma of the metempsychosis finds no expression in the rite itself, it is yet introduced in the verses." Pattanatta Pillei, a poet of peninsular India, is supposed to express the following lines[55] while torching the funeral pyre where her mother committed sati:

"1. In what future birth shall I see Her, who for then months, burdened, bore me; and when she heard the word Son, lovingly took me up in her rosy hands and fed me from her golden breast?

"2. Shall I Kindle the flame to consume Her, who for three hundred days of weariness and longing, morn and evening imploring Siva's grace, was borne down by me a burden?

"3. Shall I place Her on the pile and Kindle it,—Her who in the cradle, on her bosom, on her shoulder, caressed me, fanned me, singing soothing lullabies?

"4. Shall I put the rice into that mouth, my mother's, with which she was wont to call me her honey, necitar, her only wealth, her boy?

"5. Shall I heap up rice on the head of Her, and place the firebrand with unflinching hand and steady eye who softly raised me, pressed her face to mine, and called me of her son?

"6. Sorrow for my mother Kindles the fire, deep within, and I too have kindled the fire! See it burns! it burns!

"7. It burns! It burns to ashes—Alas! the hand which soothed me and reared me, and led me so tenderly that its touch would not have frightened away the temid biral!

"8. Is she ashes now? Hath she come already to they feet, O Siva? Hath she, evermore gazing on thee, rejoicing, forgotten me, her son?

"9. She was erewhile! She walked in the way! She was here but Yesterday! Today burned, become ashes! Come all, unlamenting, sprinkle milk, All is in Siva's power!"

Nicholas Wethington who visited India during 1612-16, describes the rite of Sati in the following words:

"Firste shee bewayleth her Husband's Death, and rejoyange that shee is nowe reddye to goe and live with him agayne, and then imbraceth her Friends, and sitteth downe on the Toppe of the File of Wood,

> and drye stickes, rockinge here Husband's Head in her lappe; and soe willeth them to sett Fyer on the Wood; which being done, her Friends throwe oyle, and divers other Things, with sweete perfumes, upon her; and she indures the Fyer with such Patience, that it is to be admired, being loose, not bounde.[56]

Rev. Mr. Lord, who was at Surat in 1731 has left an account of Sati and his observations on the practice. He writes: "The *brahmins,* as before observed leave a woman, whom her husband asks in his expiring moments, whether she is willing to follow him in death at liberty to answer either yes or no. They themselves confess, that the forcing of woman to it, either by violence or threats, is a crime that merits hell."[57] He also observes later that while the '*setreas*' (nobles) and '*Soudras*' mix something with the betel which has the property of benumbing the senses, this is not the case with the Brahmanas, for "the brahmins say they never do this, because they would have this sacrifice a voluntary one."[58]

However, Rev. Mr. Lord concludes the account by pointing out that when it comes to the actual rite "the woman goes into this hut, sits down on the funeral pile, takes her husband's head into her lap, and puts fire to it with a torch which she holds in her hand, while a great number of brahmins, with pokers in their hands, stir up the fire, which they also light on the outward part, and even push the woman forward, in case the dread of the fires should make her attempt to leap out of it; but this does not in any way correspond with the liberty which they pretend to indulge the woman in on this occasion."[59]

Col. Tod comments that the fate of the Rajput princess was one of appalling hardship. In each stage of her life death was there to claim her "by the poppy at its down; by the flame in riper years; while the safety of the interval depending on the uncertainty of war, at no period was her existence worth a twelve months purchase. The loss of the battle, or the capture of a city is a signal to avoid captivity and its horrors, which to the Rajputani are worse than death.[60] According to him, "female immolation originated with the sun-worshipping saivas and was common to all those who adored this, the most splendid object of the visible creation." The chief characteristic of this sacrifice is its expiating quality, for, by this act of faith they not only made atonement for the sins of their husbands and secured the remission of their own but "had the joyful assurance of re-union to the object whose beatitude she procured."[61] Having once imbibed this doctrine "its fulfilment is powerfully aided by that heroism of character inherent to the Rajputani."

When Jaswant died beyond the Atak, his wife, the mother of Ajit, determined to burn with her lord, but being in the seventh month of her pregnancy she was forcibly prevented from doing so. His other queen and seven concubines mounted the pyre; and "as soon as the tidings reached Jodhpur, queen Chandravati, taking a turban of her late Lord, ascended the pyre at Mundore."[62] On the murder of Ajita Simha in 1724, his six queens and fifty-eight concubines mounted the funeral pyre. "The pile flamed like a volcano, the faithful queens lived their bodies in the flame as do the celestials in the lake of Mansarovara."[63] Jaya Simha, the Mirza Raja, was also followed by some of his queens and concubines on his pyre.[64] When Raja Buddh Singh of Bundi was drowned, 84 women became Satis.[65]

Col. Tod has furnished a number of accounts of Sati and Jauhar from Rajputana. A few of the specimens would suffice. The following incident, half romantic and half tragic, belongs to the early part of the 15th Century. Sadoo, heir of the fief of Poogul in Jessulmere, was the bravest chieftain of his age. His name was a terror throughout the desert. On one occasion as he rode from a foray to his mountain home, a Rajputa invited him to his dwelling, and gave him good cheer. The daughter of the house saw Sadoo, and though she was betrothed to another; she gave her heart to the warrior of Jessulmere. Sadoo became enamoured in his turn, and before he left the house, he managed to intimate his passion. The coconut was sent and accepted, and Sadoo returned to her father's house to claim his bride. But when the marriage was over, and he was escorting her to her new home, a mortal conflict awaited him. The lover to whom she had been betrothed had sworn that he would be revenged. He encountered Sadoo, and the two chieftains fought desperately at the head of their respective followers. The bride watched anxiously from her car, but the battle was soon over. Sadoo was slain; but she had taken her resolution and did not weep a tear. The pile was prepared on the field. She sat herself thereon and took her lord in her arms. The fire was lighted; and the flames that were to have carried her to the Sun, reduced the living and the dead to dust and ashes.[66]

The princess of Kannauj, Sanyogita also committed Sati on the death of Prithviraj Chauhan.[67]

Philip Woodruff has narrated an incident at Banaras. There was a scandalous case of a widow who was "goaded by her family into the expression of a wish to burn with some relic of her husband, twelve months after her husband's death in Banaras in 1806. She jumped from the pile into the river and was rescued by a police boat. A tense situation developed which was brought under control by Charles Harding, the magistrate.[68]

When Christian missionaries started preaching their religion in India, they, first of all, wanted to remove the superstitions in Indian society—Sati being one of them. Buchanan advocated abolition of the rite by law.[69]

In November 1793 Rev. William Carey of the Baptist Mission reached Calcutta. In 1799, he saw widow-burning one evening at a place 30 miles from Calcutta. He tried to stop the ceremony and to reason with the widow and the Brahmin priests. "I talked till reasoning was of no use, and then began to exclaim with all my might against what they were doing, telling them it was shocking murder. They told me it was a great act of holiness."[70] He was greatly agitated, his spirit was in anguish, and he "Vowed... to hit this accursed thing hard, if God should spare him."[71] He sent careful investigators to every village within a radius of thirty miles of Calcutta, to learn how many widows had been immolated there in the previous twelve months, and their ages, and the children they had left behind them. "Four hundred and thirty eight was the damning total in this specific area alone, the toll of a single year's superstition, cruelty and waste."[72] The Serampore Missionaries under his leadership implored the Government to forbid the rite by law. Carey made use of his position as a lecturer in the College of Fort William to collect from the pundits there various texts from the Hindu *sastras* on which the practice of Sati was allegedly based. All these documents and statistics of sati compiled by them were placed in the hands of George Udney—a member of the Supreme Council and an ardent abolitionist himself. Udney's submission on Sati was "the first official notice regarding female immolation which had appeared in the records of the Government."[73]

Reginald Heber, the second protestant Bishop of Calcutta, was concerned with the burning of the widows, but he took a rather academic interest in the subject. One day while returning from Calcutta he saw a funeral pyre on which a widow was just burnt with her dead husband." I felt very sick at heart and regretted I had not been half an hour sooner."[74] He tried to determine the prescribed position of the widow on the funeral pyre, whether the widow was laid below the dead body of her husband as happened in this case of burning which he witnessed, or was laid by the side of dead body as the missionaries described in their account of the sati rite. He was very appreciative of the work for abolition already done by the Baptist missionaries. He invited Joshua Marshman from Serampore, expressed his concern about widow-burning, and asked his opinion on the possibility of abolition. Marshman informed him that these horrors were of more frequent occurrence within these last few years than when he first knew Bengal. According to him, the increase might be due to the increasing luxury of the higher and middle classes, and "to their expensive imitation of European habits which makes many families needy, and anxious to get rid, by any means, of the necessity of supporting their mothers, or the widow of their relations."[75] Another cause might be the jealousy of old men with young wives, who even in death, tried to cling to their exclusive possession. Marshman was strongly of the opinion that the practice might be forbidden "without exciting any serious murmurs."[76]

The Christian missionaries tried to mould the public opinion against the sati rite in both India and Britain. In Britain, Claudius Buchanan's widely-read *Christian Researches in India* (published in 1811) gave the number of widows burnt on the funeral pyres of their husbands, and William Wilberforce quoted the statistics of Satis compiled by Baptist missionaries in the House of Commons on June 22, 1813. He mentioned that in the radius of 30 miles around Calcutta, 130 widows were burnt in six months. In the year 1803, within the same space, the number amounted to 275, "one of whom was a girl of eleven years of age." He also mentioned an incident of sati witnessed by Marshman who thus concluded his dreadful experience—"The have seen savage wolves thus tearing a human body, limb from limb, would have been shocking; but to see relations and neighbours do this to one with whom they had familiarly conversed not an hour before, and to do it with an air of levity, was almost too much for me to bear."[77] Two missionary journals—The *Missionary Register* and the *Missionary Papers* circulated a series of authentic records of sati forwarded by the missionaries in India, and the latter in particular emphasized the horror of the ceremony with its vivid engravings of widows about to cast themselves into the flames.[78]

In 1810 William Ward published his *History, Literature, and Mythology of the Hindoos* (renamed afterwards a *View of the Hindoos*). In it he described some incidents of widow-burning with comments like "most shocking and atrocious murder."[79] In 1818 when Ward went to England he confirmed his accounts of widow-burning, and in 1821, on his way back to India he wrote *Farewell Letters* to friends in England

and America which he subsequently published. In these letters he presented a picture of "the superstitions of the natives, the impunity and cruelty to which they gave birth, and the moral and religious degradation they entailed." On the subject of widow-burning his letters were dramatic and effective—O that I could collect all the shrieks of these affrighted victims, all the innocent blood thus drunk up the devouring element, and all the wailings of thirteen thousand orphans."[80]

James Pegg, a former missionary of Cuttack published his *India's Cries to British Humanity,* Mr. Fowell Buxton moved a resolution in British parliament "for publication of copies or extracts of all communication from India, respecting the burning of females on the funeral piles of their husbands. On the subject of abolition he said that he was aware that a feeling of delicacy upon the superstition of the natives alone restricted the British authorities from interfering to prevent these dreadful spectacles. Still the question was not, in fact, one of religious toleration, but whether murder and suicide ought tacitly to be permitted under British Jurisdiction."[81]

From the foregoing accounts of foreign accounts of foreign travellers, merchants and administrators, some facts emerge. First, the practice of Sati was prevalent in India for more than two thousand years. Second, it was more popular among the Rajputs followed by Brahmins. Other castes followed it in rare cases.

Third, there is an element of admiration in most of the accounts. The admiration is for the extraordinary courage of widows immolating themselves, their devotion, wifely fidelity and so on.

Fourth, there is an element of condemnation for this superstition which allows murder and glorifies it in the name of custom and religion.

Fifth, a kind of drug was used in many cases to stupify the widow.

Sixth, sometimes relations and Brahmans tried to dissuade the widows from committing Sati.

Seventh, but most often there was pressure and blackmail to force the widows to immolate themselves.

Eighth, there was some speculation about the causes of this practice.

Ninth, there was some attempt to influence the public opinion and the rulers to regulate and prohibit this inhuman practice.

REFERENCES

1. Strabo, XV, 1.30 and 62, Hamilton and Falloner's translation, Vol. IV.
2. Sachau, *Alberuni's India* (London: 1914), Vol. I, p. 11.
3. Sushil Chaudhury, "A Note on 'Sati' in Medieval India," *Proceedings of Indian History Congress*, 1964 (Aligarh: Indian History Congress, 1967), Part II, Section II, p. 75.
4. *Ibn Batuta*, translated and selected by Gibb (London: 1929), p. 191.
5. Anil Chandra Banerjee, *The State and Society in Northern India* (1206-1526) (Calcutta: K.P. Bagchi & Co. 1982), pp. 194-95.
6. *Ibid.*
7. Elliot & Downson, *History of India As Told by its own Historians*, Vol. I, London, 1866, p. 6.
8. Aziz Ahmad, *Studies in Islamic Culture in the Indian Environment* (Oxford: Clarendon Press, 1964), p. 118.
9. (Rosewell, *A Forgotten Empire*, p. 129.) Quoted in M.H. Rama Sharma, *The History of the Vijayanagar Empire*, Vol. I, Bombay Popular Prakasan, 1978, p. 111.
10. (Nuniz's account is reproduced in R. Sewell, *A Forgotten Empire*, Chap. XXII). Quoted in M.H. Ram Sharma, *op. cit.*, p. 175.
11. (*India in the IV Century*, p. 68). Quoted in M.H. Ram Sharma, *The History of Vijayanagar Empire*, Vol. I, p. 63.
12. A.S. Altekar, *op. cit.*, p. 135.
13. Niccolao Manucci, *Storia do Mogor or Mogul India*, Vol. III (Calcutta: 1907), p. 57.

14. Manucci, *op. cit.*, pp. 62-63.
15. *Ibid.*, p. 147.
16. *Ibid.*, p. 148.
17. Mr. Holcombe was Deputy Governor of Vizagupatam from 1698 to 1705.
18. *Ibid.*, p. 149.
19. Ananda K. Coomaraswamy, *The Dance of Shiva* (New Delhi: Sagar Publications, 1971), p. 114.
20. *Ibid.*
21. *JASB*, 1935, p. 256.
22. William Johns, *A Collection of Facts and Opinions Relative to the Burning of Widows with the dead Bodies of their Husbands* (Birmingham: W.H. Pearce, 1816), p. 15.
23. Bernier, *Travels in the Moghul Empire* (London: 1914), pp. 363-64.
24. *Ibid.*, pp. 312-13.
25. Tavernier, *Travels in India* (Oxford, 1925), pp. 414-17.
26. William Johns, *op. cit.*, p. 2.
27. *Ibid.*, pp. 7-8.
28. R.C. Zelhner, *Hinduism* (Oxford, 1925), pp. 414-17.
26. William Johns, *op. cit.*, p. 2.
27. *Ibid.*, pp. 7.8.
28. R.C. Zelhner, *Hinduism* (Oxford: Clarendon Press, 1962), p. 147.
29. John Dawson (ed.), *Akbarnama* (Calcutta: Susil Gupta (India) Pvt. Ltd., 1959), p. 70.
30. *Ibid.*
31. *Tuzuk-i-Jahangiri*, Vol. II, translated by John Malcolm, p. 181.
32. *Ibid.*, p. 181.
33. Quoted in A.S. Altekar, *op. cit.*, p. 136.
34. *JASB*, 1935, p. 259.
35. Abbe J.A. Dubois, *Hindu Manners, Customs and Ceremonies* (Oxford: Clarendon Press, 1953) Third Edn., p. 355-67.
36. *Ibid.*, p. 355.
37. *Ibid.*, p. 356.

38. *Ibid.*, pp. 356-57.
39. *Ibid.*, p. 357.
40. *Ibid.*, pp. 357-58.
41. *Ibid.*, pp. 359-60.
42. *Ibid.*, p. 361.
43. *Ibid.*, p. 362.
44. *Ibid.*, pp. 362-63.
45. *Ibid.*, pp. 364-66.
46. *Ibid.*, p. 367.
47. Upendra Thakur, *op. cit.*, p. 171, fn. 2.
48. *Ibid.*
49. H.T. Cobebrooke, *Miscellaneous Essays,* Vol. I, p. 122.
50. H.T. Colebrooke, "On the Duties of a Faithful Hindu Widow," *The Asiatic Researches,* Vol. IV, Calcutta, 1795, pp. 209-19.
51. Quoted in J. Talboys Wheeler, *India from the Earliest Ages,* p. 394, fn. 47.
52. Quoted in Harendranath Maitra, *Hinduism: The World Ideal* (New York: Dodd, Mead & Co., 1916), p. 117.
53. J. Talboys Wheeler, *India from the Earliest Ages,* pp. 91-92, fn. 23.
54. Abbe J.A. Dubois, *Description of the People of India* (Madras: 1962), p. 221.
55. Translated by Rev. G.U. Pope.
56. Ram Chandra Prasad, *Early English Travellers in India* (Delhi: Motilal Banarasidass, 1965), p. 268.
57. William Johns, *op. cit.*, p. 10.
58. *Ibid.*, pp. 10-11.
59. *Ibid.*, p. 13.
60. Tod, *Annals,* Vol. I, pp. 215, 249, 473, 507;

    Vol. II, pp. 200, 609 etc.
61. *Ibid.*
62. *Ibid.*, Vol. II, p. 201.
63. *Ibid.*, pp. 370-71.
64. *Ibid.*, pp. 72-73.

65. *Ibid.*, Vol. II, p. 837.
66. Tod, Vol. I, pp. 627-29.
67. *Ibid.*
68. Philip Woodruff, *The Men Who Ruled India*, Vol. I (London: Jonathan Cape, 1953), p. 256.
69. Ajit Roy, "Widows are not for Burning: Christian Missionary Participation in the Abnolition of the Sati Life" in Arvind Sharma, *Sati*, op. cit., p. 58.
70. S. Pearce Carey, *William Carey* (London: 1924), p. 176.
71. *Ibid.*, p. 177.
72. *Ibid.*, p. 209.
73. Ajit Ray, op. cit., p. 59.
74. Reginald Heber, *Narrative of a Journey Through the Upper Provinces of India* (London: 1961), Vol. I, p. 47.
75. *Ibid.*, p. 48.
76. *Ibid.*
77. House of Commons *Debates*, dated 22.6.1813, Vol. V, No. 26, Col. 862, Quoted by Ajit Ray, *op. cit.*, pp. 60-61.
78. Quoted in Kenneth Ingham, *Reformers in India*, 1793-1833 (Cambridge: Cambridge University Press, 1956), p. 48.
79. Quoted in Ajit Ray, *op. cit.*, p. 61.
80. *Ibid.*, p. 61.
81. *Ibid.*

7

Protest Against Sati

It is often not realized that not only in modern, but even in ancient and medieval India, voices of protest against the custom of Sati were raised and registered. Poets, Commentators on Smrtis, Tantrikas and social reformers lent their strong voice to protest against the custom which had become popular in medieval times. Even laymen—Brahmans and relatives of the would be Satis—dissuaded them from embarking on the course. Later on Sanskrit scholars and social reformers started a crusade in the 19th Century. We propose to discuss their contributions in changing the public opinion and later influencing the government to regulate and stop this practice.

Some of the Smrti commentators are quite forthright in their criticism of the custom. Thus Medhatithi (900 A.D.) while commenting on Manu (v, 157) compares this practice to *Syenayaga* which a man performed by way of black magic to kill his enemy. He says that though Angiras allowed *anumarana* it is suicide and is really forbidden to women.[2] Just as the Veda says *'Syenenabhicaran yajet'* and yet *Syenayaga* is not looked upon as *dharma*, but rather as *adharma*[3] (vide Sabara on Jaimini, 1,1,2), so, though Angiras speaks of it, it is really *adharma*, and that a woman who is in a hurry and extremely anxious to secure heaven quickly for herself and her husband might act according to Angiras, still her action is *asastriya (not in accordance with the* sastras); besides *anvarohana* is opposed to the Vedic text 'one should not leave this world before one has finished one's allotted span of life".

Virata positively prohibits the custom of Sati. He points out that the widow can do some good to her husband, if she survives and offers him the prescribed oblations at the Sraddhan if she ascends the funeral pyre, she will be only incurring the sin of suicide.[4]

Devanbhatta, a 12th Century commentator from South India, maintains that the Sati custom is only a very inferior variety of Dharma and is not to be recommended at all.[5] Similarly Smriti Chendrika, a commentary of 13th Century says, "*anvarohana,* though recommended by the *Vishnudharma Sutra* and Angiras, is inferior to Brahmacharya (leading a celibate life), since the rewards of *anvarohana* are inferior to those of *brahmacharya.*[6]

The Tantrikas hold not only women but the female principle itself in high esteem. "Even in sacrifices, they insist, female animals should not be sacrificed. The *Mahanirvana Tantra* prescribes a whole day's fast to the man who speaks rudely to his wife, and enuoins the education of girls before their marriage.[7] The Muslim author of *Davistan* says: "The Agama favours both sexes equally. Men and Women equally compose man-kind. This sect holds women in great esteem and calls them Sakt is and to ill-treat a Sakti—that is, a women—is a crime."[8] It is not surprising, therefore, that the *Sakta Tantras* put a ban on such practices as Sati".[9] The Tantrikas asserted that "woman was the embodiment of Supreme Goddess and boldly declared that of a person burnt her with her husband, he would be condemned to eternal hell".[10] The *Mahanirvan Tantra* quite clearly condemns Sati.[11]

To the poet Bana (7th Century A.D.) belongs the credit of offering the most vehement, determined and rational opposition to the custom of Sati.[12] In the *Kadambari,* Bana expressly refers to the case of Uttara, in justification of the conduct of Mahasveta in deciding to survive her lover. Along with Uttara, Bana also gives instances of famous women like Rati, Prtha and Duhsala who did not resort to *sahagamana*. He further says:

> The custom is a foolish mistake of stupendous magnitude, committed under the reckless impulse of despair and infatuation. It does not help the dead for he goes to heaven or hell according to his deserts. It does not ensure reunion since the wife who has uselessly sacrificed her life goes to the hell reserved for suicides. By living she can still do much good both to herself by pious works and to the departed by offering oblations for his happiness in the other world. By dying she only adds to her misery.[13]

Some social reformers were also against the practice of Sati. Thus Chaitanya Mahaprabhu, denounced widow burning and recommended the remarriage of widows.[14]

In Kerala, it is believed that Shankaracharya was against the custom of Sati. A book review in *The Indian Antiquary*[15], says that the small pamphlet contains the sixty four *acharams* (rules of conduct) practised in Kerala. They are precepts given by Shankaracharya of Sringeri—one of the most celebrated teachers of Vedanta philosophy after consulting the *Dharmasastras*. They are embodied in twenty six Sanskrit slokas. These every Malyali considers himself strictly bound to attend to revere. In these acharams items 63 and 64 are relevant for us. Acharam 63 says—widows should observe the rules of Sanyasa (strict celibacy) and 64 says that there should be no Sati.

Amar Das, the Third Sikh Guru (1552-1574 A.D.) was opposed to the practice. He condemned it. The *Adigrantha* of the Sikhs says: "They are not Satis who perish in the flames, o Nanaka, Satis are those who live on with broken heart.[16]

He says, "If women appreciate their husbands they undergo sufficient pain by their death; if, on the other hand, they appreciate not their husbands, why should they be burnt?"[17] Here we have an implied reference to compulsion. Shree Swaminarayan (1781- 1830) agitated for its abolition in Gujarat by the beginning of the 19th Century.[18]

Earlier Brahmans and family members of widows dissuaded them from becoming Satis. Right from the Sati of Madri to that of Mrs. Indirabai Madhav Udgaonkar we have several instances of Brahmans and family members trying to dissuade intending Satis from embarking on their mission. Sometime they succeeded but most often they failed. Ahalyabai Holkar, who embodied the orthodox Hindu culture of the age, did not herself become a Sati, and tried her best, though without success, to dissuade her daughter from becoming one.[19] Even in Nepal and Kashmir, relations sometimes succeeded in their attempts.[20]

The native response in favour of abolition of Sati custom grew up in the early 19th Century and worked as a very effective force from inside the community. "They disputed the orthodox claim that the Sati rite was a part of Hindu religion, gave a rationalistic interpretation of the scriptures, and even under the threat of excommunication pleaded for its abolition. We know of them from the *Friend of India, the Calcutta Gazettee,* the *Bengal Harkara, the Samacara Darpana* and *the Samachar Chandrika,* from British parliamentary papers, from the speech of John Poynder at the courts of the Proprietors of East India Stock, and from the Bentinck papers".[21] In January 1820, the *Calcutta Journal* wrote:

"It is more than gratifying to find that, while the British population in India are generally speaking indifferent to the subject, there has arisen among the Hindoos themselves a powerful opposition to the continuation of these barbarous murders, and that great learning, talent, ingenuity, and moral courage have been displayed by those who endeavour to prove that even by the Hindoo laws such sacrifices are not binding; and who strenuously labour to effect their abolition".[22]

Mrtyunjaya Vidyalankar, a Brahmin of profound scholarship and of high respectability in the community, declared, after analysing the views held by different schools of Hindu law, that it was not specially enjoined in the Hindu *sastra* that the widow must burn herself and that the sati rite was purely voluntary. He concluded:

"I regard a woman's burning herself as an unworthy act, and a life of abstinence and chastity as highly excellent".

He further added: "No blame whatever is attached to those who prevent a woman's burning".[23]

His interpretation of Hindu law on Sati was well utilized by Ram Mohan Roy, who was an active social reformer. He wrote two pamphlets favouring abolition of Sati, publicised the issue widely and organised a group of opponents to Sati. The pamphlets were directed not only to his countrymen but also "to alter the notions that some European gentlemen entertain on the subject".[24]

With his deep knowledge of the Sastras, he quoted from Manu, Yajnavalkya, Visnu, Vasistha, the *Bhagavadgita,* etc. and showed that the rite of burning widows alive not only had no sanction of the higher authorities but also was contrary to their dictates. Did not the *Kena-upanisad* say that rites which had future reward for their objects were inferior religious practices? Did not the *Mundaka-upanisad proclaim* that "those fools who immersed in the foolish practice of rites, consider themselves too wise and learned, are repeatedly subjected to birth, disease, death and other pains"? The great Manu had directed Hindu widows live as ascetics. If custom or long tradition ought to set aside the precepts of the *sastra,* and should be the determining factor, as the advocates of the rite claimed, then the inhabitants factor, as the advocates of the rite claimed, then the inhabitants of the forests and mountains who have been in the habit of plunder, must be considered as guiltless of sin, and it would be improper to endeavour to restrain their habits". We had our sastra, and we had our reason. In the sastra such female murder was altogether forbidden, and our reason also declared "that to bind a woman for her destruction, holding out to her the inducement of heavenly rewards, is a most sinful act".[25]

Rammohan Roy drew upon the *Bhagvadgita,* among other

texts, in presenting his case against the practice to his co-religionists. He cites more than thirteen verses to build up his case.

Some Smrti texts which recommend Sati, do so on the argument that thereby heaven is secured by the widow. Roy counters this by invoking the doctrine of *niskama karma* of the Gita,[26] namely that action performed without desire for rewards is superior to one directed towards it and hence to be preferred. A Sati is a reward-oriented act, aimed at securing residence in heaven, it is an inferior form of action and, therefore, to be discouraged. Roy cites the Gita II, 49; III, 9; V, 12; XII, 10-11; and XVIII, 6 in support of his position.[27] Thus the final conclusion on the subject is to the effect: "That rites are not prohibited but that pious works performed without desire are preferable to works performed for the sake of fruition; and he who performs those works without desire, is superior to him who performs works for the sake of fruition". Once this conclusion is drawn,

Roy drives home his point:

> "If then works without desire are acknowledged by you to be superior to works with desire of fruition, why do persuade widows to perform work for the sake of fruition, and do not recommend to them rather to follow asceticism, by which they may acquire eternal beatitude ?"[28]

But the opponents have two objections:

> First, even if the widow followed asceticism, she might fail and hence it was beller to commit Sati.

Secondly, even the practice of asceticism leads to heavenly rewards, hence there was no difference between the two options.

Roy counters these objections by citing the *Gita* (II, 40). He argues that there is really nothing like failure on the spiritual path where even a little goes a long way. To the second objection he says that while it is true that both (performers of desire- free and desire- oriented deeds) go to heaven, the similarity ends there and their fates diverge thereafter. Those whose actions were motivated by desire enter the world of mortals, after a spell in heaven. He cites the *Gita* (IX, 21) to support his point. But their spiritual mobility remains unimpeded. Here he quotes *The Gita* (VI,41):

> The opponents argue that women are only entitled to the inferior path of action and not of asceticism. But Roy quotes the *Gita* (IX, 32) where even those of base origin, women, men of the artisan caste, serfs, etc. are guaranteed salvation.[29]

Thus, Roy used the *Gita* to forensic affect. In one passage he asks his opponents rhetorically:

> "The *Gita* is not a rare work, and you are not unacquainted with it. Why then do you constantly mislead women unacquainted with the Sastras, to follow a debased path, by holding out to them as temptations the pleasure of futurity, in defiance of all the sastras, and merely to please the ignorant?"[30]

One of the followers of Roy in his movement against the custom of Sati was Gourisankara Bhattacarya, the editor of a Bengali weekly, *Sambada Bhaskar.* He was an independent and forceful writer and a keen supporter of widow remarriage and girls' education. The *Calcutta Courier* wrote about him, "Being freed from his trammels of Hindoo superstition, he gladly embraces every opportunity of exposing the folly of his bigoted countrymen". He pleaded with Bentinck for the abolition of the rite, though its advocates threatened to excommunicate him from society. In 1849 he wrote in one of his editorials: "If I could oppose directly and without fear the big bosses of society in advocating the abolition of concremation, then nothing would deter me from expressing myself freely".[31]

Another active supporter of the abolition of this rite was Kalinath Roy Chowdhary of one of the most ancient and honourable families of Bengal. He led a delegation of Hindus to congratulate the Governor General (Bentinck) for promulgating the Regulation banning Sati. The orthodox Hindus expelled him and his associates from the society.[32]

Other notable figures in the anti-sati movement were Dwarkanath Tagore and Prasanna Kumar Tagore, Munshi Mathuranath Mullick, Rama Krishna Sinha, and Anandaprasad Bandyopadhyay. Bishop Heber quoted Marshaman "...among the laity many powerful and wealthy persons agree, and publicly express their agreement, with Rammohan Roy, in reporting the custom".[33]

A vigorous press campaign against the Sati rite was also launched through three journals—*The Sambada Kawmudi,* the *Samacar Darpana* and *the Bangadoot*. By 1826 the attention of the English educated Bengali youth was drawn to the subject. Letters appeared in the *Bengal Harkara* (in January and February 1826) denouncing the Sati rite and all those who encouraged it, and urging the Government to take effective measures to prevent the practice.[34]

REFERENCES

1. Arvind Sharma et al., *Sati* (Delhi: Motilal Banarasidass, 1988) p. 15.
2. पुंवत्स्त्रीणामपि प्रतिषिद्ध आत्मत्यागो यद्यप्याङ्गिरसे पतिमनुम्रियेरन्नियुक्तं तदपि नित्यवदवश्यं कर्तव्यम्। फलस्तुतिस्तत्रास्ति फलकामायाश्चाधिकारे श्येन-तुल्यता। तथेव श्येनेन हिंस्यादभूतानीत्यधिकारस्याति प्रवृद्धतरद्वेषान्धतया सत्यामपि प्रवितो न धर्मत्वम, एवमिहापि अतिप्रवृद्धफलाभिलाषायाः सत्यपि प्रति-षैधे तदतिक्रमेण गरणे प्रवृत्युपपत्रेर्न शास्त्रीयत्वमतोसत्येव पतिमनुमरणेऽपि स्त्रियाः प्रतिषेयधः।। किंच 'तस्माद् ह न पुरायुधः प्रेयात्' इति प्रत्यक्ष भूतिविरोधीयम।

   Medhatithi on Manu V, 157.
3. नैव श्येनादयः कर्तव्या विज्ञायन्ते । यो हि हिंसितुमिच्छेत्तस्यायमभ्युपाय इति तेषामुपदेशः। श्येनेनाभिल्यजेतेति हि समामनन्ति नाभिवरितव्यमिति।

   Sabar on Jaimini, 1,1,2.

   See P.V. Kane, *History of Dharmasastra* Vol. II, Part I (Poona: Bhandarkar Oriental Research Institute, 1941), pp. 631-32.

4. अनुवर्तते जीवन्तं न तु यायान्मृत पतिम्।
जीवद्भर्तृहितं कुयन्मिरणादात्ममधातिनी।।
Virata, Quoted by Apararka on Yaj.; 1, 87.

5. A.S. Altekar, *op. cit.*, p. 124.

6. यत्तु व्रिष्णुना धर्मान्तर मुक्तं मृते भर्तारि ब्रह्मचर्यं तदन्वारोहनं वा.......
तदेतद्धमन्तिरमपि ब्रह्मचर्यधर्माज्जधनयम्। निक्रृष्टफलत्वात्।
स्मृतिचन्द्रिका, व्यवहारकांड,

7. Arvind Sharma, *op. cit.*, pp. 16-17.

8. T.M.P. Mahadevan, *Outlines of Hinduism* (Bombay: Chetana Ltd., 1960), p. 205.

9. *Ibid.*

10. A.S. Altekar, *op. cit.*, p. 125.

11. भर्त्रा सह कुलेशीनि न देहत्कुलकामिनीम्।
तव स्वरूपा रमणी जगत्याच्छन्नाविग्रहा।
मोहाद्भर्तुश्चितारोहाद् भवेन्निरयगामिनी।।
Mahanirvanatantra, X, 79-80.

12. A.S. Altekar, *op. cit.*, p. 124.

13. यदेतनुमरणं नाम तदतिनिष्फलम्। अविद्वज्जनाचरित एष मार्गः। मोहविलासितमेतद्ररभसोचरितामिदं यदुपरते पितरि भर्तरि भ्रातरि वा प्राणः परित्यज्यन्ते। स्वयं चेन्न जहति न परित्याज्याः। उपरतस्य तु न कमपि गुणामावहति। न तावदुस्यायं क्रुभत्योकोपार्जनहेतुः न निरयपातप्रतिकारः, न परस्पर-समागमनिमित्तम। अन्यामेव स्वकर्मफलपाकोपषितामसो अवशो नीयते भूमिम।

असावपि आत्मधातिनः केवलमनसा संयुज्येते। जीवंस्तु जलाज्जलिदानादिना बहूपकरो-त्युपरतव्यात्मनश्च मृतस्तु नोभ यस्यापि।
Kadambari, Purvardha (Bombay: Nirnayasagar Press, 1910), p. 308.

14. J. Talboys Wheeler, *India from the Earliest Ages*, p. 382.

15. *Keralacharam* (Calicut: Collectorate Press, 1866) reviewed by S. Sankunni Wariyar, in *The India Antiquary,* Vol. IV (August 1875), pp. 255-56.

16. Upendra Thakur, *op. cit.*, p. 161.
Cf. A.S. Altekar, *op. cit.*, 131.

17. Mecauliffe, *The Sikh Religion*, Vol. II (Oxford, 1909), p. 228.
18. Raymond Brady Williams, *A New Face of Hinduism: The Swaminarayan Religion* (Cambridge: Cambridge University Press, 1984), pp. 21-22, 143.
19. A.S. Altekar, *op. cit., p. 140;*

    See also Ep. Circ, IV, Hg. No. 18 regarding the Sati of Dekabbe where her parents dissuade her from becoming Sati.
20. See *Rajtarangini* and Nepal inscriptionin this regard.
21. Ajit Ray, "Widows are not for Burning: Native Response to the Abolition of the Sati Rite," in Arvind Sharma, Sati, *op. cit.*, 49.
22. *Calcutta Journal*, dt. 20.1.1820.
23. *Friend of India* (Monthly series, Oct. 1819, pp. 473-76) quoted in Ajit Roy, *op. cit.*, p. 50.
24. Rammohan Roy, *The Practice of Burning Widows Alive* (Calcutta: 1818), Advertisement.
25. *Ibid.*, p. 96.
26. T.M.P. Mahadevan, *op. cit.*, p. 186.
27. Arvind Sharma, *op. cit.*, p. 68.
28. Ram Mohan Roy, *Translation of a Conference Between an Advocate for and an opponent of, the Practice of Burning Widows alive from Original Bungla* (Calcutta: Ram Mohan Roy, 1818), p. 111.
29. *Ibid.*, p. 112.
30. *Ibid.*, p. 106.
31. *Sambada Bhaskara*, dt. 26.5.1849 (translated from original Bengali by Ajit Ray and quoted in Ajit Roy, *op. cit.*, p. 53.
32. Ajit Roy, *op. cit.*, p. 53.
33. Reginald Heber, *Narrative of a Journey Through the Upper* Provinces of India (*London: 1961)*, Vol. I, p. 48.
34. Ajit Roy, *op. cit.*, p. 53.

8

Regulation and Prohibition of Sati

Even the Muslim rulers endeavoured, as much as they could, without offending their Hindu subjects, to regulate and prevent the practice of Sati. Muhammad Tughlaq tried to stop this practice.[1] Humayun wanted to prohibit it in the case of the widows, who had passed the child-bearing age.[2] He, however, could not take any adequate steps in the matter. Akbar allowed liberty of conscience in so far as that liberty did not endanger the lives of others. He gave a marked example of this in his dealing with the Hindu rite of Sati. The custom had been so long prevalent among Hindu ladies of rank that not to comply with it had come to be regarded as a self-inflicted imputation of the chaste life of the widow. Still, the love of life is strong, and the widow, conscious of her own virtue, unwilling to sacrifice herself to an idea, had occasionally shown a marked disinclination to consent to mount the Pyre. It had often happened then that the priests had applied to her a persuasion, either by threats of the terrors of the hereafter of the application of moral stimulants, to bring her to the proper pitch of willingness. Such deeds were abhorrent to the merciful mind of Akbar, and he discouraged the practice by all the means in his power. His position towards the princes of Rajputana, by whom the rite was held in the highest honour, would not allow him so far to contravene their time-honoured customs, which had attained all the force of a religious ordinance, to prohibit the self-sacrifice when the widow earnestly desired it. Before such a prohibition could be issued time must be allowed, he felt, for the permeation to the recesses of the palace of the liberal principles he was inaugurating. But he issued an order that, in the case of a widow showing the smallest disinclination to immolate herself, the sacrifice was not to be permitted. Badaoni quotes the order of Akbar: "If a Hindu woman wished to be burnt with her husband, they should not prevent her, but she should not be forced against her will."[3] In the 22nd year of his reign Akbar translated his opposition to the custom into action by appointing inspectors to see that no force was used to compel widows to burn themselves against their will. He personally persuaded a young girl to refrain from becoming a Sati but he did not succeed. He called the girl before him and offered wealth and protection but she refused to be comforted, refused his persuasion and insisted on committing Sati. Akbar was forced, though reluctantly, to give his consent to the sacrifice, but sent his son Daniyal with her who continued to dissuade her from her resolve. She did not yield.[4] Akbar did not content himself with words only. Once, when in Ajmer, while his confidential agent Jai Mall (son of Mal Deo and nephew of Raja Bihari Mall of Ambar) was on a mission to the amirs of Bengal, news reached him that Jai Mal, had died of sunstroke in the vicinity of Chausa. Jai Mall had been a great favourite with Akbar, for of all the Rajputana nobles he had been the first to pay his respects to him, and had ever rendered him true and loyal service. He had married a daughter of Raja Udai Singh of Jodhpur, a princess possessing great strength of will. When the news of her husband's death reached Ambar, she positively refused to become a Sati. Under the orders of the Emperor Akbar she had an absolute right to use her discretion. But when she used her discretion, the outcry against her headed by her son became so uncontrollable, that it was resolved to force her to the stake. Information of this reached Akbar and he decided to prevent the outrage. His feeling of justice and humanity made him fear that if he sent messengers to stop the proceedings; some delay might occur, so he mounted his horse and rode with all speed to the place. As the facts were not fully known, some of these men, in their thoughtlessness, were disposed to resist and make disturbances. But when His Majesty (Akbar) arrived, Jagannath and Rai Sal came forward to meet him, and brought the leader of these foolish men to him. He accepted their assurance of repentance and only placed them in confinement.[5]

Jehangir also tried his best to follow the footsteps of his illustrious father in this respect, and he is said to have prohibited Sati performed without prior royal permission, especially in the cases of young widows whose marriage had not been consummated.[6] The people of Rajour (near Kashmir) were Muslims at the time of Jahangir. It is said they were Hindus whom Sultan Firuz converted to Islam. But they were still called Rajas. Jehangir in his Memoirs[7] observes that they still had "the marks of the times of ignorance. One of those is that just as some Hindu women burn themselves along with their dead husbands, so these women (the Rajour Women) are put into the grave along with their dead husbands. I heard that they recently put alive into the grave a girl of ten or twelve along with her dead husband who was also of the same age".

Jahangir condemned this practice among the local Muslims and issued a decree that "hereafter they should not do such things, and whoever was guilty of them, should be capitally punished."

Emperor Aurangzeb appears to have taken a stern step in this direction. We learn from Manucci that the emperor, on his return from Kashmir (December 1763 A.D) issued an order that in all lands under Mughal control never again should the officials allow a woman to be burnt.[9] A.S. Natarajan writes "following the rescue of a widow from the flames at Agra, Aurangzeb rejected a petition of the Brahmans and decreed that in all lands under Mughal rule never again should officiate allow a woman to be burnt".[10]

However, this much is certain that those wishing to become Satis had to obtain a special license from the governors of the Mughal provinces. It might have acted as a deterrent. Tavernier, a 17th Century traveller, narrates how a widow of 22 went to the governor of Patna to get his permission, and how she held her hand in the flame of a torch till it was burnt to cinders in order to convince the officer that she was a willing party, and was not afraid of the fire.[11] A similar case has been narrated by Sir Frederic Halliday.[12] Here also a widow resisted all dissuasion, and finally proved her determination by asking for a lamp, and holding her finger in the flame until it was burnt and twisted like a quill pen, all this time she gave no sign of fear or pain whatever. Sir Frederic Halliday had, therefore, to grant her wish."

That the need for permission became part of the procedure seems evident from incidents occurring even among Indian Communities living outside India "In 1723, the widow of an Indian merchant in Moscow asked permission to be burnt alive alongside her husband on his funeral pyre. Her request was refused. At once all the Indian factors disgusted by this act, decided to leave Russia, taking their wealth with them. Faced with this threat, the authorities gave in. The incident was repeated in 1767."[13] This provision for obtaining a special license reduced the incidence of Sati but did not materially check the custom, as the prescribed permission could be usually obtained without much difficulty.[14] However, the author of *Travels of Peter Mundy* says that the practice had become rare in his time as a special license from the ruler or governor had to be obtained under the Mughal[15].

After capturing Goa one of the first acts of Alfanso de Albuquerque was to abolish Sati in 1510[16].

The French in Chandernagore, the Danes in Serampur, the Portuguese in Goa had prohibited Sati. Hindu residents in these areas had to take their widows into British territory and to get a British magistrate's sanction before burning them.[17]

Towards the beginning of the 19th Century, the Brahmin government of Poona and the Maratha government of Savantwadi had issued official orders, definitely disapproving and discouraging the custom.[18] Maratha rulers had "by a wise neglect, which neither encouraged by approval nor provoked by prohibition, rendered the practice very rare" writes Sir John Malcolm.[19]

One of the Indian practices that scandalised the British from the earliest days was the practice of Sati or widow-burning. Nevertheless, they adopted the policy of non-interference with the religious and social customs of the natives. According to V.N. Dutta,[20] the rite of Sati most probably received its first official mention in 1787, when Sir Charles Malet, the resident at Poona, enclosed an account by Mr. Cruso of a Sati which took place in Poona in 1786. In 1789, Mr. M.H. Brooks, Collector of Shahabad (Bihar) wrote in the course of a letter to Lord Cornwallis, that in spite of its policy of non-interference in religious matters, the government should prohibit a practice "at which humanity shattered."[21]

Thereafter, from time to time, a few magistrates in the Bengal Presidency reported their success in persuading young widows to desist from immolating themselves. They also continued to ask for rules for their guidance, especially when the woman was being coerced into immolating themselves. They also continued to ask for rules for their guidance, especially when the woman was being coerced into immolating herself after being stupefied with drugs. The government at Fort William approved of the successes, advised administrators to use only persuasion and did not give any specific directions.

In 1805 Lord Wellesley, Governor-General of India, formally asked the court of Nizamat Adalat whether Sati could be abolished and recommended that administering intoxicants to widows be prevented and that women who were not capable of judging for themselves, be resumed.

The Pandit scholar consulted by the law officers of the

Nazamat Adalat replied that Sati was founded on the religious texts of Hindus and was expressly stated in their law. There were, however, certain circumstances in which the woman could not commit Sati; if she were pregnant, prepubescent, the mother of an infant (unless some one offered to look after it), in a state of uncleanliness, or stupefied with drugs. Most important, the Sati had to be entirely voluntary which required that the woman should have taken the decision completely on her own without any external influence.

Though this opinion was received in 1805, the government did not formulate its policy on this practice till 1812 when it declared that like all other religious practices, sati should be allowed where it was countenanced by religion and prevented where it was forbidden. The distinction was thus made between legal and illegal Sati; however cautiously. The Government defined a Sati as illegal when the woman was: (a) Under compulsion, (b) intoxicated, (c) pregnant or (d) had a child under three whose nurture was not undertaken by another.[22]

The government directed its officers to remain present at a sati and prevent illegal satis form taking place. Officers were also directed to admonish the relatives of the woman that they would be dealt with as common criminals if they took one further step towards effecting their criminal and illegal designs.

It may be pointed out that the concept of voluntary and legal Sati was intelligible and (however barbaric they found it) acceptable to the British government. They were attacking not the practice but its abuses and irregularities. Secondly, when the Sati woman herself.

Thus a distinction between legitimate and illegitimate Sati was made and police officials were made responsible for the observance of the sastric injunctions. As these were mostly Hindus and Muslims living under the prevailing system, the perversion of official orders was inevitable, and it was taken by the people to mean official sanction to Sati.

In the words of H. Oakley, Collector of Hooghli:

"Police offices are now ordered to interfere, for the purpose of ascertaining that the ceremony is performed in conformity with the rules of the sastras, and in that event to allow its completion. This is granting the authority of Government to the burning of widow; and it can scarcely be wondered at that the number of sacrifices should have doubled when the sanction of the ruling power is added to the recommendation of the sastras".[23]

A category of illegal satis that had been omitted from the circular was that of brahmin widow; the practice of *Anumaran* was not permitted to brahmins; they were only allowed *Sahamaran*. *Anumaran* for a brahmin widow was irregular according to the shastras and was therefore illegal as per the governement's broad policy, though it was not specifically mentioned as such in the circular.

The new directions of the government did not meet with any spectacular success. It is estimated that during 1813-16 only ten illegal satis were prevented out of a total of 400 that occurred in the presidency of Bengal. Amongst the illegal sati were six girls between the ages of eight and twelve.

In 1817 the government policy on Sati was reconsidered. In September 1817, at the government's directions, the Nizamat Adalat prepared a draft of the second sati circular, in order to rectify the shortcomings of the first. Religious authorities were quoted in the preface which showed that the *Shastras* did not permit Sati. For the first time the government made a move that challenged the religious sanction behind sati.[14] On the practical side, circumstances that constituted an illegal sati were clarified and enlarged and, in one case, even removed. Thus, widows under fifteen, brahman widows who burnt separately from the husband in *Anumaran*, non-brahman widows who did not burn immediately after hearing of the death of the husband and widows who wished to postpone the sati to a later date were declared illegal. Only a legally married widow was acknowledged to have the right to commit sati on the other hand, the Circular clarified that if a woman's child was over four years of age, there was no need for any one to undertake to look after it before she could legally commit Sati.

Some important additions were made in this draft circular. The relatives of the widow were required to give notice of Sati to the police. Magistrates were authorised to convict all those who neglected to give this information, with fine and imprisonment. The police were required to read out the rules to the widow in the presence of witnesses and secure their signatures. If the sati were illegal the police, the relatives and other persons present were required to prevent the sati and if the still took place, the relatives were to be held liable to a criminal prosecution.

The Nizamat Adalat's recommendations were too radical for the government. In particular the government objected to two sections: section XII made any injury or degradation to a widow punishable by fine or imprisonment. It also afforded protection to the widow who withdrew at the last moment, and sought to punish any relatives who maltreated her. Section XV specified that any property that may have devolved on the widow after her husband's death would be at the disposal of the government, if she was burnt or buried alive.

The government rejected both sections on the interesting ground that they were not prepared to interfere with the family life and property of the widow! The rest of the draft of the Nizamat Adalat was promulgated by the government as a circular in 1817.

The circular had no impact on incidents of Sati. In fact the number of satis increased form 378 in 1815 to 839 in 1918. In 1821, M.C. Smith, second judge of the Sudder Adalat, declared roundly that confusion prevailed, but that on the whole the impression was that the government was more favourable to sati than otherwise. The Government was more favourable to sati than otherwise. The Governor-General had reluctantly to admit that the circular order had tended to augment rather than diminish the frequency of these sacrifices. The returns for the years between regulation and prohibition in the Bengal Presidency were:

1815	:	378 Satis Officially reported
1816	:	442 Satis Officially reported
1817	:	707 Satis Officially reported
1818	:	839 Satis Officially reported
1819	:	650 Satis Officially reported
1820	:	598 Satis Officially reported
1821	:	653 Satis Officially reported
1822	:	583 Satis Officially reported
1823	:	575 Satis Officially reported
1824	:	572 Satis Officially reported
1825	:	639 Satis Officially reported
1826	:	518 Satis Officially reported
1827	:	517 Satis Officially reported
1828	:	463 Satis Officially reported

Right through about 60 per cent of these occurred in the Calcutta division, where often the presence of European magistrates and sometimes of horrified English ladies, kindled the crowds to an intoxication of delight.[25]

From 1818 onwards, the British in India not allowed to forget Sati. Apart from the raging controversy in Calcutta, servants of the company were pressing for a lead from the government. Lord Amherst had sought the views of English functionaries, and had consoled himself for inaction with their against suppression.

However, with the arrival of Lord Bentinck as Governor-General of India, a new and decisive phase started. On 12 June, 1829, Bentinck wrote to Astell, the Chairman of the Board of Directors, East India Company—

"There cannot be a man more anxious for the abolition

of that horrible rite than my self. I do not believe that among the most anxious advocates of that measure any one of them feel more deeply than I do, the dreadful responsibility hanging over my happiness in this world and the next, if, as the Governor-General of India, I was to consent to the continuance of that practice for one minute longer".[26] The agony of a humanitarian gradually turned into the determination of an administrator.

He started wider consultations with the Judges of the Nizamat Adalat, the police Superintendents, various public functionaries, military officers and Indian reformers.

Lord William Bentinck, in his minute to the Board of Directors dated November 8, 1829, set out very conscientiously the various prevailing views on the subject and his own reasons for agreeing with, or rejecting, them. He first refers to the views of Mr. Horace Wilson, distinguished orientalist, that once the Indians—through the suppression of Sati—begin to suspect, "that it is the intention of the British Government to abandon this hitherto inviolate principle of allowing the most complete toleration in matters of religion that there will arise in the minds of all so deep a distrust of our ulterior designs that they will no longer be tractable to any arrangement intended for their improvement, and that the principle of a purer morality, as well as of a more Virtuous and exalted rule of action, now actually inculcated by European education and knowledge, will receive a fatal check".[27] He agrees with Horace Wilson that it would be a dangerous evasion to argue that the practice is not an essential part of the Hindu religion; he accepts that the "conscientious belief of every order of Hindus, with few exceptions, regards it as sacred". He accepts that an attempt to put down the practice will inspire extensive dissatisfaction. But he disagrees that the dissatisfaction would manifest itself in outbreaks and revolts. He bases this confidence on the habitual submission of centuries to the will of the ruling power, the rich landed proprietors of the permanent settlement being deeply interested in the continuance of the British Dominion, and absence of the practice among those in the army. I, therefore, at once deny the danger in toto, in reference to this part of our territories where the practice principally obtains".[28]

Bentinck analyses the opinions of 49 officials. Five are against any direct interference with the practice; twelve favour abolition but oppose absolute and direct prohibition under the authority of the Government; eight favour abolition by the indirect interference of Magistrates and other public officers; and twenty four favour total and immediate suppression. He makes a pointed reference to the reported demands for such an act by the Supreme Court.[29]

As we have seen, Bentinck had ascertained the opinion of the judges and officers of the Government but had no way of ascertaining native Indian opinion on the question of abolition of Sati. He had, however, heard of Rammohan Roy as an advocate of the abolition of Sati and sought a meeting with him. The manner in which this came about was thus "narrated by Rev. Dr. K.S. Mac Donald, at a meeting in 1879, on the information supplied to him by Ananda Chandra Basu, the oldest pupil then living of Rammohan".[30]

"Lord William Bentinck, the Governor-General, on hearing that he would receive considerable help from the Raja in suppressing the pernicious custom of widow-burning, sent one of his *aides-de-camp* to him expressing his desire to see him. To this the Raja replied, "I have now given up all worldly avocations, and am engaged in religious culture and in the investigation of truth. Kindly express my humble respects to the Governor-general and inform him that I have no inclination to appear before his august presence, and therefore I hope that he will kindly pardon me". These words the *aide-de-camp* conveyed to the Governor-General, who enquired, "I told him that Lord William Bentinck, the Governor-General, would be pleased to see him". The Governor-General answered, "Go back and tell him that Mr. William Bentinck will be highly obliged to him if he will kindly see him once". This the *aide-de-*

camp did and Rammohan Roy could no longer refuse the urgent and polite request of his lordship.

After describing the views of Horace Wilson, William Bentinck wrote in his minute referred to earlier.[31] "I must acknowledge that a similar opinion as to the probable excitation of a deep distrust of our future intentions was mentioned to me in a conversation by that enlightened native, Rammohan Roy, a warm advocate for the abolition of Sati and of all other superstitious and corruptions engrafted on Hindoo religion, which he considers originally to have been a pure Deism. It was his opinion that the practice might be suppressed quietly and unobservedly by increasing the difficulties and by the indirect agency of the police. He apprehended that any public enactment would give rise to general apprehension, that the reasoning would be, while the English were contending for power they deemed it politic to allow universal toleration and to respect our religion, but having obtained the supremacy their first act is a violation of their profession, and the next will probably be, like the Muhammadan conquerors, to force upon us their own religion".[32]

In the final peroration, Lord Bentinck struck a high note the first and primary object of my heart is the benefit of the Hindoos. I know nothing so important to the improvement of their future condition, as the establishment of a purer morality, whatever their belief, and a more just conception of the will of God. The first step to this better understanding will be dissociation of religious belief and practice from blood and murder. They will then, when no longer under this brutalizing excitement, view with more calmness acknowledged truths. They will see that there can be no inconsistency in the way of providence, that to the command, received as divine by all races of men, "No innocent blood shall be spilt," there can be no exception; and when they shall have been convinced of the error of this first and most criminal of their customs, may it not be hoped that others which stand in the way of their improvement may likewise pass away, and that, thus emancipated from those chains and shackles upon their mind and actions, they may no longer continue, as they have dome, the slaves of every foreign conqueror, but that they may assume their just places among the great families of mankind. I disown in these remarks or in this measure any view whatever to conversion to our own faith. I write and feel as a legislator for the Hindoos, and as I believe many enlightened Hindoos think and feel."[33]

Thus Bentinck was aware that both the Directors and Parliament desired the discontinuance of Sati. Also that section of the English public which took any interest in Indian affairs would support him in his measure to suppress the Sati rite. The moral responsibility of the government became a physical possibility because Indian opinion also supported the measure. Thus Christian missionaries, Rammohan Roy and his associates and English public opinion helped Bentinck who was determined to do some good work to clear himself from the blame of Vellore mutiny. "Bentinck realized that it would be foolish even of a man with better memories of Vellore to miss the opportunity while a strong native response for abolition was sweeping over the country. And he acted".[34] Frenderick John Shore in his *Notes on Indian Affairs* wrote afterwards that the tide of opinion in India was so strongly opposed to Sati rite that any Governor-General would have acted as Bentinck did.[35] However, the credit goes to Bentinck to show his determination after so much vacillation on the part of his predecessors.

Thus the Sati Regulation Act of 1829(XVII) was enacted after much consultation within and without the government. It was called 'A Regulation for declaring the practice of Suttee or burning or burying alive, of the Widows of Hindus, illegal, and punishable by the criminal courts'. Thus the Act was a major departure on the previous policy on Sati; it was intended to punish all Satis as criminal acts. There was no more any distinction between a legal and illegal Sati. Section I of this Act stated 'the practice of Sati; or of burning or burying alive the widows of Hindus, is revolting to the feelings of human nature; it is no where enjoined by the religion of the Hindus as an imperative duty....'. Thus the general policy of non-interference with the religious and social customs of the natives could be reconciled with the need to prohibit and punish Sati.

Section-2 declared Sati to be illegal and punishable by the criminal courts. Under Section 4, a sentence for culpable homicide was imposed on all persons involved in the Sati regardless of the voluntary nature or otherwise of the Sati. Under Section 5, the Nizamat Adalat was empowered to enhance the punishment to death Sentence if the accused were found guilty of using violence or compulsion, or intoxicants upon the woman".[36]

The draft of the Indian penal Code prepared mainly by T.B. Macaulay during 1833-38, again reintroduced the nefarious distinction between voluntary and involuntary sati. In his draft, clause 298 defined voluntary culpable homicide by consent. It read, Voluntary culpable homicide is 'voluntary culpable homicide by consent when the person whose death is caused being above twelve years of age suffers death or takes the risk of death by his own choice.' The consent would be valid only if (a) coercion was not used, (b) the consent was not given while being unable to exercise one's choice or judgement on account of intoxication, passion or derangement, (c) no deception was exercised and (d) no material facts were concealed.

Macaulay's draft thus reintroduced the distinction between voluntary and involuntary sati. Perhaps he bowed to the pressures of liberalism which required tolerance for other religions. In 1846 the Third Law Commission speculated on the reasons that night have led their predecessors to distinguish between voluntary culpable homicide and voluntary culpable homicide by consent, and concluded that the distinction must have been made because of the need to allow for the practice of sati. In the even, Exception-5 to section 300 of the Indian Penal Code incorporated Clause 298 with one change: the age of consent was raised to eighteen years.[37]

Stray incidents of Sati were reported even after its prohibition by Bentinck and occasional cases occur even now. After such a case in 1986, strong protests were made by Women's organizations, some intellectuals and the media.

The clamour that went up from all including the Joint Action Committee Against Sati and the Sativirodhi Sangharsha Morcha was for a separate legislation to punish Sati, its glorification and monetary and political exploitation. There was also some discussion whether sati was voluntary or involuntary. Activists took the stand that no sati can be voluntary. Even if physical force or drug was not used, coercion and blackmail were. The spectre of an unhappy and dishonourable life loomed over the widow and might have made a horrible death to a living one.

Some of the activists pleaded that involuntary sati was covered by Indian Penal Code and was treated as murder. At the most an amendment to section 300, Exception 5 declaring that in no case of Sati the consent of the victim would be valid would have sufficed. A separate law against glorification and exploitation would be necessary. But this plea was ignored. In fact "so unqualified and blind was the faith in the written word that while damning the government of India and Rajasthan for their inaction—for not implementing the existing law—the universal cry was for another law.[38]

The Rajasthan Legislative Assembly was in session and the government did not want any problems on the floor. Many opposition leaders of Bhartiya Janata Party and Janata Party were supporters of the Sati. Some Congressmen were also sympathetic to it. So the Assembly was prorogued for a day and the Ordinance was signed on 1.10.87 by the Government on the grounds that the Assembly was not in session! The Rajasthan Legislative Assembly passed the Bill on 10th November 1987.

After the promulgation of the Ordinance in Rajasthan demands were made and writs filed in the Supreme Court to direct the Union Government to enact a similar law. The

Central Government passed the law in mid-December by extending the session of Parliament. It was done in hot haste without consultation with the people.

Both the Act, define Sati. Sec. 2(c) of (The Commission of Sati (Prevention) Act, 1987 (Central Act) says:

"Sati" means the burning or burying alive of

(i) any widow along with the body of her deceased husband or any other relative, or with any article, object or thing associated with the husband or such relative;

or

(ii) any women along with the body of any of her relatives, irrespective of whether such burning or burying is claimed to be voluntary on the part of the widow or the woman or otherwise Section 3 provides for the punishment. It says "Whoever attempts to commit sati and does any act towards such commission shall be punishable with imprisonment for a term which may extend to one year or with fine or with both." It is noteworthy that for the first time the rescued woman is liable to punishment.

Even this law is not satisfactory. The glorification of sati is made illegal but will it have retroactive effect? The abettors are given more punishment than the woman which is against principles of criminal justice. The burden of proof is on the victim which is very dangerous. Who will give evidence in favour of the woman and admit his completely and become liable for tougher punishment. Legal language is not enough in these matters.

REFERENCES

1. Upender Thakur, *op. cit.*, p. 161.
2. *Journal of Asiatic Society of Bengal*, 1935, p. 76.
3. Badaoni, II (Lowe), p. 388.

4. Ananda K. Coomarswamy, *The Dance of Shiva* (New Delhi: Sagar Publications, 1971), p. 114.
5. *Akbarnama*, ed. John Dowson (Calcutta: Susil Gupta (India) Pvt. Ltd), 1959, p. 70; Cf. G.B. Malleson, *Emepror Akbar* (New Delhi: Asian Publication Services, 1978), pp. 165-66.
6. Withington, p. 219 quoted in P.N. Ojha, *Glimpses of Social Life in Mughal India* (New Delhi: Classical Publications, 1979), p. 69.
7. *Tuzuk-i-Jahangiri*, Vol. II, tr. John Malcolm. p. 181.
8. *Ibid.*, p. 181.
9. Manucci, *Storia*, II, p. 47.
10. A.S. Natarajan, *A Century of Social Reform in India* (Bombay: Asia Publishing House, 1959), p. 25.
11. Tavernier, *Travells in India*, Oxford, 1925, pp. 414-417.
12. Ananda K. Coomarswamy, *op. cit.*, p. 115.
13. F. Braudel, *The Wheels of Commerce*, New York, 1979, Quoted in Romila Thapar, "In History," *Seminar*, Feb. 88, p. 17.
14. A.S. Altekar, *Position of Women in Hindu Civilization*, p. 133.
15. *Travels of Peter Mundy*, Hakluyat Society, 1914; quoted in Upendra Thakur, *op. cit.*, p. 171.
16. N.M. Penzer (ed.) *The Ocean of Story* Vol. IV (London: Chas J. Sawyer 1925), p. 263.
17 A.S. Natarajan, *op. cit.*, p. 26.
18. A.S. Altekar, *op. cit.*, pp. 140-41.
19. Quoted in A.S. Natarajan, *op. cit.*, p. 25.
20. V.N. Dutta, *Sati: a historical, social and philosophical enquiry into the Hindu rite of Widow burning* (Manohar Books, New Delhi, 1988).
21. Upendra Thakur, *op. cit.*, p. 175.
22. Vasudha Dhagamwar, "Saint, Victim or Criminal," *Seminar*, February, 1988, pp. 34-35.
23. Natrajan, *A Century of Social Reform in India* (Bombay: Asia Publishing Houe, 1959), p. 29.
24. Vasudha Dhaganwar, *op. cit.*, p. 35.
25. Natarajan, *op. cit.*, p. 30.

26. Bentinck's minute; in Demetrius Charles de Kavanagh Boulger, *Lord William Bentinck* (Oxford: Clarendon Press, 1892).
27. Upendra Nath Ball, *Ram-Mohan Roy* (Calcutta: U. Roy & Sons, 1933), p. 97.
28. S. Natrajan, *op. cit.*, pp. 31-32.
29. *Ibid.*, p. 32.
30. Upendra Nath Ball, *op. cit.*, p. 92.
31. *Ibid.*, pp. 92-93.
32. *Ibid.*, pp. 97-98.
33. S. Natarajan, *op. cit.*, pp. 33-34.
34. Ajit Roy, *op. cit.*, pp. 33-34.
35. *Ibid.*
36. Vasudha Dhagamwar, *op. cit.*, p. 36.
37. *Ibid.*, p. 36.
38. *Ibid.*, p. 36.

9

Sati After Bentinck

As we have seen, the Regulation of 1829 prohibited the practice of Sati and, when challenged, the Act was upheld by the privy council. The enactment of the legislation soon told on the custom which gradually lost the popular sanction and became almost extinct. Apart from the British territory, the prohibition of Sati was made a feature of the treaties between the then Imperial Government and the Indian States. Nevertheless, occasional cases of Sati are still reported. "Age-old superstitions and prejudices die hard. Man's vanity and prejudices some times assume extraordinary shapes which defy rigorous laws and checks, for social reforms must come from the bottom, and not from the top and only then they produce the desired results which are effective and lasting".[1] Sati was no doubt banned by regulation and was made punishable but its fading glory and halo still haunted men's mind and they could not fully do away with it. It is, therefore not surprising that occasional cases of Sati are still reported.

On the death of Ranjit Singh in 1839 A.D., inspite of the implicit injunction against this measure in Sikhism[2] and the Act of 1829, four queens and seven concubines mounted his funeral pyre. During the troublesome period following his death, princes and generals fell in quick succession and almost everyone of them was accompanied by his wives and concubines. Three women died with Maharaja Kharag

Singh, five with Basant Singh, 11 with Kishori Singh, 24 with Hira Singh and 310 with Suchet Singh.[3]

Jung Bahadur, the Prime Minister of Nepal, used his influence in vain to prevent this practice. But on his death in 1877 several women burnt with his corpse.[4] In Berar (Hyderabad) in spite of the promulgation of the orders issued by the Nizam in 1847, a Hindu woman after the death of her husband immolated hersalf ignoring the prohibition of the Deshmukh. The Resident there Upon requested the Nizam to enforce the orders which he had formerly issued. After a good deal of correspondence between the Resident and the Nizam's *Peshkar*, a second order was issued.

That, however, was of no avail and the Resident was mortified to receive now and then intimation of the occurrences of Sati from various parts of Hyderabad.[5]

Even after its prohibition in British India in 1829, the custom of Sati continued to linger in Rajputana, its greatest stronghold, for some years. At the deaths of Maharana Jiwan Singh of Udaipur in 1838 and Maharaja Man Singh of Jodhpur in 1843, several women mounted the funeral pyre. Jaipur agreed to prohibit the custom in 1846 and other Rajput States gradually followed. Udaipur was the greatest stronghold of the orthodox Rajput tradition and the last public case of a legal Sati took place there in 1861 at the death of Maharana Sarup Singh. But even the Rajput public opinion had changed by this time. Not a single legal wife of the Maharana committed Sati. Ultimately a slave girl was persuaded to accompany the great Sisodia Chief.[6]

In 1862, a wandering Bhat and beggar died in a village at Jodhpur (Rauputana). His wife aged twenty two, was not with him at the time but arrived at the village one evening six days afterwards, accompanied by her brother-in-law (husband's brother). She then learned for the first time that her husband was dead, and at once declared her intention of becoming Sati; but she is said to have been dissuaded by her husband's relation, and to have retired for the night. In the night her brother-in-law heard her moving and saw her collecting wood for a funeral pyre. He assisted her and when the pyre was ready, the woman seated herself on it and her brother-in-law set it on fire. In the morning the people of the village saw the blaze and on closer view found that the woman had burnt herself to death.[7]

Smt. Nayan Tara Sahgal, daughter of Smt. Vijaya Lakshmi Pandit and Jawaharlal Nehru, has given an interesting story of this custom. Her great-grand-mother Gopika, mother of eight sons and five daughters, was the last of the Marathi women of the Village to commit sati.[8]

Two cases were reported in the Gaya District of Bihar in 1901 and 1903. In June 1913, wife of Ramlal (a Brahman) of Jaranli Village of Mainpuri district of U.P. committed Sati.[9] In this case her relations were convicted for abetment to suicide.There was an abetted Sati case in November 1929 at Barh (Patbna district of Bihar) and in 1930 a widow in Hazaribagh district attempted to immolate herself.[10] A.S. Altekar has given an account of the Sati of his own sister in January 1946. Smt. Indirabai Madhav Udgaonkar showed "an indescribable fortitude in carrying out her long-formed and oft-announced resolution not to survive her husband when on 17.1.1946 she committed herself to flames with in 24 hours of her husband's death, in spite of the pressing entreaties of all her relations. Nothing, not even the presence of a sucking child, would dissuade her from taking a step which she believed to be dictated by her duty and Dharma as a *Pativrata*".[11]

After independence also some cases have been reported. The following illustrations would indicate that the practice, though illegal, is not yet completely dead:

(a) An 18-year old Rajput girl became Sati in the Village of Bamauri, near Lalitpur, in the Jhansi district, following the death of her husband.

The National Herald[12] reported that "despite persuasions by her relatives, it is said, she remained adamant and marched with the funeral procession and sat down on her husband's pyre and was consumed by the flames:

"It is reported that the girl's father and brother-in-law have been taken into custody by the police".

(b) *The Statesman*[13] reported yet another case in 1954 from Jodhpur (Rajputana). According to this report the Pujari, who performed the funeral rites of the late Brigadier Zabbat Singh, comptroller of the Jodhpur Maharaja's household, when his widow committed *Sati,* has been arrested under sec. 306, I.P.C. (Indian Penal Code abetment of suicide).

"A party of Journalists who motored down to Sir Pertap Singh's Thada, found hundreds of people still offering coconuts and going round the spot where the cremation took place.

"Later, Inquiries made at the residence of the Late Brigadier revealed that after her husband's death on the evening of October 18, the Thakurani appeared determined to die. She did not allow anybody in the room and sat through the night her husband's head in per lap chanting 'Rama, Rama....".

"Just after the Brigadier's death she had bedecked herself in her marriage jewellery and dress. She then gave one of her to her son and wished him all happiness.

"No one could tell, probably for fear of the police investigation as to how she managed to accompany the body in the truck up to the cremation ground and who lit the pyre.

"Anti-police slogans were shouted by hundreds of people when the police went to the cremation ground the next morning to collect the remains of the couple for investigation.

(c) In 1954 Taradevi committed Sati in a village, Madhavka-vas (Rajaputana). This case has been described in some detail by Sudesh Vaid.[14]

The official family version is that Taradevi made up her mind to mount the funeral pyre at the suggestion of her dying husband. "On his death, she did not shed any tears and personally chose to a site for the cremation on family land near the entrance to the village, in front of which runs a railway line. She dressed herself in bridal finery, asked that information of the impending immolation be spread in the village, and led the procession. She also personally instructed the pundit in the performance of various rituals. The procession was accompanied by band-baja and her relatives, carrying swords, 'protected' her during the procession and at the cremation site. The bier was carried by minor children of the family and the Sati asked the two-year old son to touch the pyre which lit itself. A few hours before fer death, Taradevi miraculously bestowed a well on the village. She raised her hand and a well sprang up in the courtyard. Thousands flocked to see the young women's immolation, a bazar sprang up, a temple trust was immediately formed. An annual fair is held at that place since 1955, for which an otherwise unscheduled stop of the train facilitates the devotees and traders. The temple and rooms for pilgrims were funded by Rajputs and businessmen. The ex-rulers of Jaipur and Jodhpur, along with important politicians, have visited the marble temple and lent support to its activities.

Taradevi's three brothers-in-law and the pundit who performed the *havan* wre arrested shortly afterwards, but no one was convicted. Reportedly, handcuffs fell off the offenders' wrists three times, the son of the S.I. fell ill, and the sati appeared in a dream to warn him against 'harrassing' her relatives. The local police and officer and the D.M., 'awed' by these sundry miracles, themselves reversently worshipped the 'sacred' spot. An unbeliever among the railway officials was immediately sent a divine warning through a minor accident on the railway tracks. Taradevi's mother in a dream asked her daughter how she could have borne the pain of live burning. The daughter replied with serenity that she had not suffered at all, the fire was like bathing in water, an *agnisnan* and so on and so forth.

Sudesh Vaid is not inclined to accept this version in toto. In fact, he feels that in this particular case, inheritance appears to be the underlying motive. The perpetrators of the crime well knew that it is illegal and hence due care was taken to have monors perform a crucial part of it. Taradevi's father-in-law's land was equally divided among his four sons each getting 100 bighas. Before that event, some land had already been allocated to tenants under the land reform laws. The choice of the site not only secured a certain amount of land from government appropriation, but also secured it for Taradevi's children, and for her childless sister (her sister-in-law, too), who became their guardian. On Taradevi's death, the inheritance of two brothers could thus be consolidated for the single son and heir, and family disputes averted. Notably, the maternal uncle who played a pivotal role in setting up the temple, nominated the infant son as its sole

(D) In August 1980, a 35-year Brahmin widow, Hardei committed sati at a village Palson, P.S. -Govardhan of Mathura district of U.P.[16]

Hordei (now sati Hardevi) was a woman of 35 years having 5 children, 2 daughters and 3 sons. She belonged to a middle class Brahmin family and was the wife of the second son of Khusiram Sharma. Her husband died of cancer at the age of 38. The family version of the story says that Hardevi, though just literate, was a pious lady and used to recite the Ramayan, especially Sundar Kand of it. She was a devoted and obedient lady. Before her husband (Radheshyam Sharma) died at about 2.30 P.M. on 16th August, 1980, she put on her finest attire and ornaments and sat near him. When he died, she moved 5 times round his dead body and sat down. She did not weep, rather she asked others also not to weep. Then she recited the Ramayan. People were making preparations for the cremation, When the procession started, she led it keeping the Ramayan on her head. When the pyre was ready, she made 21 rounds of the pyre, she sat on it and placed the head of her husband in her lap. Then she declared her resolve to become Sati.

Family members were reluctant to light the pyre. The Sati assured them that fire would appear automatically and began prayers. The news spread like wild fire and hundreds of people gathered there. By 6 in the evening the police party led by Gyaneshwar Sharma (S.I. of Govardhan P.S.) reached the spot. He persuaded her to leave the pyre but she was adamant. SDM also failed to persuade her.

Then the women constables lifted her from the pyre and persuaded her to consult a Sadhu of Mathura, who knew the procedure of Sati custom. She was admitted to hospital and case of attempted suicide was instituted against her.

On 18th August she was released on bail on the prayer of her father-in-law. Two constables were deputed to watch her and prevent her from becoming Sati. She cried and wept in the night and gifted away her belongings in the morning of 19th August. Then she went to a temple and sang bhajans there. At about 1.30 P.M. a Sadhu came to the temple and conferred with her in private. Then he disappeared.

Then Sati came home, bathed and did her hair. Then she sat on the pyre which was cold by now. The news spread all around and hundreds of people began to shout "Sati Mata Ki Jai" (Hail to mother Sati). She went round the pyre 21 times and rubbed her hands and lo and behold fire was produced. People put, sesamum, ghee, coconut etc. on her and she was burnt in no time. The constables on duty expressed their helplessness and said that as she was going bare handed and the pyre was extinguished, they felt assured that she could not do anything. But it was a miracle and so on and so forth.

Later on the D.M., S.P. and MLA reached there and almost every body accepted that it was a miracle. The D.M. formed a Committee to look after the spot and the offerings on the pyre.

It was also declared by the father of Hardevi that she remembered previous two berths. She was the daughter of a she pherd, and then was born in a Jatava family.

Ultimately she was born in an Ahivasi Brahmin family. But Govind Singh, author of the piece in *The Nutan Kahanian* does not seem to accept this version. In his opinion, it was a well planned conspiracy hatched by her family members. She had a death-wish, no doubt, she preferred death to a life of misery in a joint family. Taking advantage of her mental condition her family members instigated her to commit Sati when she was in police lock up she was released on bail by her father-in-law. The whole village collected barley, ghee, sesamum, coconut etc. to burn her. She had ghee in her hand which she rubbed in her sari and used a matchstick. The family wanted to build a temple of Sage Saubhari and the Sati to collect funds to earn money. The story of shepherd and Jatava births were spread to mobilise opinion in the village which consists of Brahmans, Jatavas ani shepherds. The police and magistracy connived at this incident.[17]

(E) Earlier a sati case was reported from a village of Jaipur which occurred on 8th November 1961.[18]

(F) In U.P. a Sati case was reported in August 1981.[19]

(G) In 1987 the famous case of Jyoti Kunwar occurred in Deorala (Rajasthan). An 18-year old Rajput girl named Jyoti Kunwar mounted the pyre of her husband at Deorala village on 4th September 1987. It is alleged that she was drugged. Even if it be false, the fact is that her family members did not prevent her from mounting the pyre, rather the whole village gathered there and it was made a spectacle.[20]

The Sati Dharma Raksha Samiti (SDRS) has released figures of Satis which says that there have been only 28 cases since 1947.[21]

In fact, most of the cases of Sati in post-independent India have been reported from Rajasthan and Western U.P. The Sekhawati region has witnessed a deliberate and organised effort to revive the practice of widow immolation. At present the region consists of Sikar and Jhunjhunu districts of Rajasthan, but both culturally and administratively, it earlier embraced a wider territory.

What is notable is that during neither the medieval nor the colonial period was this region particularly known for this practice.[22]

The present revival has been led by the three upper castes of the areas—the Rajputs, the Agarwals and Brahmans. The significant role of Brahmans, Bhats and Charans may not be very overt at present. The Brahmans as priests and the Bhats and Charans, as bards and genealogists, were important social groups who invested widow immolation with heroic valour and religious merit. The former gave it religious sanction while the latter gave it a place within the 'glories' of family history and Rajput 'Custom' and tradition.[23]

The relationship of these groups to the Rajput rulers was not simply one of dependence. They were landowners due to the extensive practice of making land grants to temples and to individual priests and bards. On these three castes rested the legitimacy of the power of the Rajputs. Apart from their role in the political sphere, they were important in the social sphere and in family life. They regulated and maintained clan and caste superiority, arranged matrimonial alliances and played a determining role in the lives of women, particularly the Rajput, both at the material and ideological levels. The ideology of Rajput male valour was the combined making of these groups, with all its prescriptive implications for Rajput women—namely to uphold its feminine counterparts—Jauhar and Sati. The investing of Sati with material valour was carried, via Todd's romantic narratives of such events, to the Indian middle classes in other parts of the country and has formed a staple of Hindu cultural nationalism from the late nineteenth Century to the present times. After the abolition of princely states and the Zamindari and jagirdari system, these caste groups are no longer in a position to exploit other groups as in pre-independence days. However, through caste and family networks, they are lending support to the revival of the practice of Sati. It is not accidental that the so-called living Sati at Devipura (prevented in 1985) asked instructions from a guru at Triveni temple located at a stone's throw from the village, that a guru from the same temple was also associated with a Sati at Hathideh (1977) or that a priest who officiated at the Sati at Jhadli (1979) and wrote booklets in honour of the 'Sati mata' had links both with the Hathideh family and the Triveni temple. It may be noted that Deorala is in the vicinity of this temple.[24]

The businessmen (Bania-mahajans) were close to the durbar and as financiers and administrators, had various honorific titles conferred on them by the rulers. Further, due to the *ijara* system they had a firm base in the agrarian economy. Astraders, moneylenders and bankers they were close to village level thakurs. Both the ruler and thakurs wooed them to set up commercial centres within their territory, there by creating a network among them within the entire region. The colonial period gave a tremendous boost to the fortunes of both impoverished banias and rich mahajans. The opening of the Delhi-Calcutta railway route in 1860 saw thousands of Agarwals from this region spread all along the Gangetic belt to U.P., Bihar, Assam, Bengal, Orissa and further into Burma and parts of South-east Asia. Calcutta soon became the headquarters of Marwari capital amassed through cotton, jute, oilseeds, and opium trade as well as through banking and speculation. As is well known, the Burrabazar area of Calcutta, which recently saw demonstrations and a bandh cell by pro-sati Marwaris, is the business locality dominated by traders from this and other areas of Rajasthan.

The Shekhawati traders prospered with the advent of independence and now head some of the leading industrial and business houses of the country. Among them are the Jhunjhunwalas, the Khaitans, the poddars, the Kanodias, etc. They maintain links with Shekhawati through the huge Sati temples they have set up in the region.[25] With the abolition of princely states and zamindari and Jagirdari system after independence, the social and economic powers of Rajputs were threatened. Some of them have joined the army and police forces. The military and police service gives them a sense of continuing their 'martial' tradition as Kshatriyas. This middle class leadership was recently able to mobilise thousands of small peasants rights to the soil. The leaders addressed tens of thousands of lathi and sword-bearing saffron-clad Rajputs with exhortations to remember that their ancestors had fought for 'dharma' and that their women had committed Jauhar. Thus the small jagirdars and *bhoomias* fought their economic and social interests through the ideology of erstwhile Rajput ruling class. They claimed for themselves the 'heritage' constructed by local bards and by nationalist historians—of Rana Pratap, Mewar, Chittor, of the 'heroic Rajput', committing Jauhar and Sati'.[26]

Recent Satis in the area have tended mainly to come from impoverished families in strained circumstances. The victims were burnt by the in-laws, the ntal family was not informed. The *sasural*-family is abetted by the *mukhia* and elites of the locality. What makes Sati different from the other related crime of burning a daughter-in-law, is that the murder is a public event, 'endowed' with erligious sanctity, invoking the 'Kshatriya tradition' of heroic death and 'glorious Hindu womanhood'. Through it emerges a reinforcing of *Pativrata dharma*. in the hagiographical accounts constructed about the Sati, the victim is made into an exemplar of a dutiful, pious daughter and daughter-in-law and symbol of conjugal love and sacrifice.[28]

Sudesh Vaid concludes his piece with the following observation:

> The present iconography of Sati in the area, the *trishul*, embodies the convergence of several interest groups and ideological currents—assertions of a 'glorious' Rajput communal identity, aspirations to Kshatriya status by the business community, militant Hindu revivalism, the attempt to have he gemonec control by the upper castes—all fuelling a reassertion of patriarchal norms for women. Hence the fury of the onslaught against those who protest the

mystification of this crime. The well-orchestrated propaganda emanating not only from the Dharm Raksha Samiti but from a wide spectrum of Pro-sati ideologues in the press and the universities attests to the deep stakes —economec, social, cultural—that the reveved practice of Sati in the Shekhawati region has for the post-colonial upper and middle class in rural and urban India.[29]

REFERENCES

1. Upendra Thakur, *op. cit.*, pp. 176-77.
2. The Sikh Guru Amar Das was Opposed to this practice. However when they developed into a fighting community, they adopted this custom like other Kshatriyas as a symbol of martial traditions.
3. A.S. Altekar, *op. cit.*, p. 132.
4. Upendra Thakur, *op. cit.*, p. 177.
5. "Sati in Hyderabad," *Proceedings of Indian History Congress*, 1953, pp. 341-43.
6. A.S. Altekar, *op. cit.*, pp. 141-42.
7. J. Talboys Wheeler, *India of the Veidc Age*, pp. 70, fn. 23.
8. Nayantara Sahgal, *Prison and Cholocate Cake*, Cf. Vijaya Lakshmi Pandit, *The Scope of Happiness: A Personal Memoir*, (London: Weidenfeld and Nicolson, 1979), p. 77 refers to this incident "Ranjit's (Nayantara's father') great-grand-mother became a sati on the death of her husband. A banayan tree was planted on the site of her immolation, and to this day the village people and the passing traveller bow reverently before it."
9. Ramdial Vrs Emperor, AIR (1913), 36, Allahabad.
10. *Bihar Through the Ages*, pp. 682-83.
11. A.S. Altekar, *op. cit.*, p. 137.
12. *The National Herald*, Lucknow, dt. 12.6.1954.
13. *The Statesman*, Calcutta dt. 25.10.54.
14. Sudesh Vaid, "Politics of Widow Immolation," *Seminar*, Feb. 1988, pp. 22-23.
15. *Ibid.*, p. 23.

16. The report is based on coverage in *the Swaraja Times & the amar Ujala* (Hindi daily of Agra) of August 1980, and *the Nutan Kahanian* (Hindi monthly, Allahabad, No. 80).
17. Govind Singh, "Hardevi Sati ya Balika Bakra?", *The Nutan Kahaniyan*, Allahabad, No. 80, pp. 87-88.
18. *The Searchlight*, Patna dt. 14.11.1961.
19. *The Times of India*, Delhi dt. 13.8.81.
20. *The Times of India*, Delhi, dt. 6.9.87.
21. *The Seminar*, Feb. 1988, p. 26.
22. The Sekhawat Chieftains paid tribute to the Amber (Jaipur) rulers. There are few instances of burning of Ranis and other women on the death of Amber rulers. One of them even tried to abolish the practice. Jaipur was the first state of Rajputana to abolish Sati in 1846. At that time leading Sekhawati chieftains had given their public approval to the abolition legislation.
23. Sudesh Vaid, *op. cit.*, p. 21.
24. *Ibid.*
25. *Ibid.*
26. *Ibid.*, p. 22.
27. *Ibid.*, p. 23.
28. *Ibid.*
28. *Ibid.*

10

Causes of Sati

(1) As we noticed earlier, there was a belief in pre-historic times that the needs of the dead in the next world are more or less similar to those in this life. Hence the surviving relations deemed it their in this life. Hence the surviving relations deemed it their pious duty to provide him all that he needed in this life. His wife, weapons, horses, servants were sent with him. This practice was prevalent in Scythian, Greek, German, Slav, Egyptian, Thracian, Indian, Chinese, Japanese and many other societies. Especially the warriors & Kings & noblemen were honoured in this way. Traces of this system continued in India also.

(2) During the Indo-European age it was followed among the Gauls, the Goths, the Celts, the Norwegians, the Thracians, the slaves etc. Hence the inference may be justified that it was well established among, the Indo-Europeans. The reference in *Atharvaveda* also shows that it was prevalent among the Aryans before they entered India.

(3) The Bahlikas & Madras followed this practice in Warrior families.

No one quite knows why sati seems to increase after the establishment of British Raj in Bengal. The following explanations have been offered:

(1) "This increase is apparent rather than real. That the cases were more carefully reported, and not that more actually occurred."[1]

(2) It is due to epidemics. More people died, hence number of Sahis also increased.[2]

(3) The "unknown reason" for increase in Sati after the British occupation of Bengal may be due to the popular mistaking of the British policy of non-interference in traditional practices as British approval there of. So the Court of Directors thought anyway.[3]

(4) Joshua Marshman, a beading Baptist missionary of Serampore informed Reginald Heber that these "horrors" were of more frequent occurrence with in these last few years (early 19th Century) than when he first knew Bengal. The increase according to him, might be due to the increasing luxury of the higher and middle classes, and "to their expensive imitation of European habits which makes many families needy, and anxious to get rid of, by any means, of the necessity of supporting their mothers, or the widow of their relations."[4]

(5) Another cause might be the jealous of old men with young wives, who even in death, tried to cling to their exclusive possession.

(6) P.V. Kane has suggested that the prevalence of *Dayabhag* School of Hindu law in Bengal, according to which a widow could inherit the share of her husband in joint family property, was one of the main reasons of increasing number of Satis in Bengal. He writes:

It appears from all accounts of travellers and others that Widow-burning prevailed more in Bengal during the centuries immediately preceding its abolition than anywhere else in India.[5] If that was so, there were certain good reasons for that state of things. In the whole of India except Bengal, the Widows of members in a joint Hindu family are only entitled to maintenance, and have no other right over the property of the family. In Bengal, wherever the Dayabhag prevails, the widow of a sonless member even in a joint Hindu family is entitled to practically the same rights over joint family property which her deceased husband would have had. This must have frequently induced the surviving members to get rid of the widow by appealing at a most distressing hour to her devotion to and love for her husband..... The figures given in *Suttee* lend support to the view expressed here, since Benares, where the rights of widows were insignificant, was responsible for a small number of *Satis* only".[6]

(7) Another reason appears to be the system of Kulinism in Bengal. The *Kulin* Brahmins (Brahmins of high social status) used to have multiple wives. Kulinism was the practice by which it was socially possible for even a hundred women to be given in marriage to one Brahmin by reason of his *Kul* (high social status). Many members of the four highest clans in Bengal made a profession of marriage, writes Edward Thompson, selling themselves as husbands to a number of women, few of whom ever lived with their husbands or even saw him after marriage, except when they climbed the funeral pyre. Widows were subjected to a life of enforced austerity and subjection if they refused to immolate themselves; "there were not wanting men prepared to go the length of dragging them to the funeral pyre and thus compelling co-cremation".[7]

The unsympathetic attitude of society towards the custom of widow remarriage and a general dislike of the peculiar custom of self-immolation by widows. N.K. Dutt says "the introduction of Suttee is only a logical corollary to the total prohibition of widow marriage and the maintenance of a high standard of womanly chastity."[8]

Alberuni thought that its popularity was due to the ill-treatment of the widows and in the case of widows of royal household, it was virtually forced to prevent them from doing any thing unworthy of their family.

Bana relates how the captive wives of the defeated kings gad to serve and attend on queen Yasovati, queen of Prabhakarvardhan. Yasovati narrates to her son Harsha the great honour and glory that was hers, she refers to the fact that the wives of the enemies defeated by her husband waved chowries over her.[9] The lot of the wives of conquered kings and warriors was most miserable in all countries including India. Vengeance for the truculence of their husbands was wreaked on the poor wives by carrying them as captives and making them work as slaves. Manu[10] allows a soldier to retain women conquered by him along with other booty. Hence apprehension of humiliation and servitude made them prefer self-immolation to survival.

The custom of Satidaha originated among the princely order in the early part of the beginning of the Christian era. It was considered to be the best proof of the affectoin and attachment of the wife for her dead husband. In later days among the Rajputs it became a prevalent custom for which they felt very proud of their womenfolk who threw themselves into the burning pyre of their dead husbands willingly and gracefully. Those who deviated from this practice were considered to be neglecting in their duty and insulting the memory of the dead man".[11]

In a narrow view the rite was an Indian practice, byt in a wider view the rite was the local development of a custom practised in some form or other over a wide area of the world—in Slavonic lands, Scandinavia, Greece, Egypt, China, etc.[12] The original cause of the custom might be the jealousy of men over women. The native oppenents to the sati rite pointed out that the cause of such a practice was "excessive jealousy of their female connections operating in the breasts of Hindoo Princes... They availed themselves of their arbitrary power, and under the cloak of religion introduced the practice of burning widows alive".[13]

"Jealous men once invented the Chastity belt for their wives to wear when they went on long journeys. But for the longest jouney—the journey to eternity from where there is no return—they decided to take their wives with them so that they could rest in peace in their tombs".[14]

Bengal and Rajasthan were the strongholds of this practice, and castewise, the institution seems to have been confined to the high caste, and in particular Kshatriyas and Brahmins. This leads M.N. Srinivas,[15] the noted Indian sociologist, to speculate:

> "In view of the face that the two areas of concentration of sati are in northern India, one is tempted to ask whether it was tied up with the institution of hypergamy, and the incidental phenomenon of polygyny at the top of the hypergamous hierarchy".[16]

With regard to the rise in the incidence of Sati in Bengal in early decades of the nineteenth Century Marshman had noted that it was probably due to the emulation of expensive European habits by natives, and to the jealousy of old men with young wives.[16] Srinivas[17] says, "What is significant in Marshman's explanation is the effort to explain one social phenomenon sudden rise in sati—by reference to other social phenomena. Only through research into the conditions obtaining in Bengal in the first two decades of the 19th Century will make clear whether there is any substance to Marshman's explanation".

Srinivas further comments:

> "There is a still deeper level of explanation of Sati which needs to be adumbrated here. Between the end of the Vedic period and 12th Century A.D., the

idea seemed to have gained ground that the husband should have exclusive and total control over his wife's sexuality. Pre-pubertal marriage was the surest way to make certain of it. Pre-pubertal marriage also transferred the responsibility for safe-guarding the girl's sexuality from her male kin in her natal family to her husband and his agnates. Once married, total faithfulness was expected of the wife, and this was attemted be be assured by the deification of the husband. Total control over her "sexuality was not only for the duration of the marriage; it extended to the pre- and post-marital periods, absurd as it may seem to outsiders. Virginity in brides was ensured by pre-pubertal, and frequently child marriages, while celibacy was required of the widow. She was disfigured by having her head shaved, and by forbidding to her the symbols of the happy and auspicious state of sumanglihood (i.e., the married state with the husband alive), and her activities were restricted to the Kitchen and to ritual. She was condemned to perpetual mourning, as it were, and she became a symbol of inauspiciousness and ill-luck. The death of her husband was attributed to the sins she had committed in a previous incarnation. The widow who decided to commit sati was, on the contrary, the mirror image of the widow who had decided to live. She was auspicious, and she was dressed as a bride for her last journey. Her martyrdom brought good reputation and good luck to her kinsfolk and to her village. In some parts of India, memorial stones were erected to Satis.

"While the widow and sati were treated so radically diffferently, the ruling idea in both the cases was the assertion of the dead husband's total control over the wife's sexuality. The wife, on the otehr hand, had no such exclusive right over the husband's sexuality. Not only was a widower not required to burn himself on his dead wife's funeral pyre, he was urged to marry soon.... This one-sidedness is really the key to the relationship".[18]

The *Satidaha*[19] illustrates the psychological complexity surrounding Sati. We are told that women used to be attracted to the act of sati for the following reasons:

1. Deep love for the husband.
2. Veda, Purana, Sastra and Smrtis have extolled the greatness of a sati, and women believe in this.
3. The desire to enjoy pleasures for 30,000 years(?) upon feeling the husband through the act of Sati from all sins.
4. The hope of attaining infinite pleasures upon momentary agony of being burnt by the fire of the funeral pyre.
5. A relief from harsh suffering on account of the deprivation of sex in widowhood.
6. Aspiration for renown, i.e. inclusion in the list of the god satis whose names are chanted as a form of morning worship.
7. The common belief of Hindus that life is transient and therefore detachment towards life should be cultivated.

To those women who volunteer to perform sati after the death of their husband, the following thoughts and anxieties occur.

1. It is futile for a woman to continue mundane existence after the husband is dead.
2. The love for children can never match the love for the husband.
3. Now she must be a refugee in the same household in which she had been a mistress concerning every last detail. As a refugee she is bound to go through the sufferings of widowhood, and finally to die.
4. It is better to be peaceful forever after momentary endurance of the flames than remain a wresched widow for many years. After all, every one has to

> face death someday. So why miss the auspicious occasion of obtaining heaven by following this way (performign sati)? Many good women of the past like us have offered up their lives in the funeral pyre on such occasions. So why should we fear?

This is the psychology of women who volunteered to perform Sati.[20]

One prevalent view is that self-immolation of widows was necessitated by the Muslim invasions when Rajput and other upper caste women resorted to it to defend their honour from Muslim marauders. The prevalence of this practice in medieval Rajputana and Vijaynagara is ascribed to this reason. But this view is not supported by historical evidence. One a few cases in Rajputana can be accounted for on this score. The princess of Vijayanagara had been married with great pomp and splendour to the Bahmani sultan. The princess of Amber was united with the Mughal emperor Akbar in holy wedlock. The leading princely families of Rajputana were favourites of Mughal rulers, yet they practised Sati. Inscriptions from the peninsula refer to women becoming satis when their husbands died in battles fought between the among Hindu rulers such as the CHalukyas, Yadavas and Hoysalas, in the period from the tenth to the fourteenth Centuries A.D. Many of these inscriptions are located in Maharashtra and Karnataka.

The peak period of Sati in these areas was pre-Islamic in that Muslim invasions were not the cause. Howevr, when faced by Turkish armies from the end of the thirteenth Century, the earlier ritual would have continued. The greater incidence of Sati in Bengal was also not caused by Muslim invasions. Thus this theory is not supported by historical evidence.

Another view is that sati was prevalent in Kshatriya or warrior families. Others also adopted it to seek Kshatriya status. Thus it was a case of Sanskritization whereby lower castes adopt the values and customs of upper castes to rise higher in the social hierarchy. Most of the sati inscriptions refer either to families of Kshatriya status or those seeking such a status. One of quoted inscription of the eleventh century refers to a Sudra woman whose husband died in battle against the Ganga ruler and who, despite strong opposition from her parents became a sati. Her husband held a high military position under Chola control. Her insistence may hae been occasioned, among other things, by the wish to establish status. The custom was prevalent at this time among those who held high administrative and military positions generally associated with Kshatriyas. Therefore it is likely that members of lower castes holding similar positions emulated the style of the Kshatriyas.[21]

The notion of bride-prince can suggst in some situations the purchase of a woman, the logical termination of which may have been the requirement of her dying together with her husband, although this is not typical of bride-prince. But perhaps a more acceptable explanation may relate to societies changing their systems of kinship and inheritance.

Thus a number of factors accounted for the practice of sati. No single cause can be ascribed for the prevalence of this custom for so long in India.

REFERENCES

1. W.J. Wilkins, *Modern Hinduism* (London: T. Fisher Unwin, 1887), p. 390.
2. Edward Thompson, *Suttee* (London: George Allen and Unwin, 1928), p. 73.
3. Michall Edwards, *British Idnia* (New York: Taplinger Publishing Co., 1967), p. 101.
4. Reginald Heber, *Narrative of a Journey Through the Upper Provinces of India* (London: 1961), Vol. I, p. 48.
5. Edward Thompson, *op. cit.*, pp. 69, 72.
6. *P.V. Kane,* op. cit., p. 635.
7. S. Natrajan, *op. cit.*, p. 26.
8. Sukla Das, *Socio-Economic Life of Northern India* (New Delhi: Abhinav Publications, 1980), p. 93.

9. आपीतौ युष्मद्रिधैः पुत्रैरमित्रकलत्रबन्दीवृन्द विधूयमानचामरमरू चलचीना-शुकधरौ पयोधरौ। हषचरित, 5

   Harsa Charita, V.

10. *Manusmrti*, VII, 96.

11. M.L. Bhagi, *Ancient India—Culture and Thought* (Ambala Cantt. n.d.), p. 37.

12. C.H. Tawney (Tr.), *The Ocean of Story* (London: 1924), Vol. IV, Appendix I.

13. *Calcutta Gazettee*, dt. 18.1.1830. Letter of Hindus to Bentinck. Quoted in Ajit Roy, *op. cit.*, p. 56.

14. Ajit Roy, *op. cit.*, p. 56.

15. "Foreword" to Arvind Sharma, et. al, *Sati*, p. XI.

    Cf. S. Natarajan, *op. cit.*, p. 25.

    Natrajan says: "Only in Rajasthan and Bengal in the British sphere of influence did Sati persist on a large scale. And there the evil was aggravated by the prevalence of the custon of multiple wives among Rajput princes and Kulin Brahmins."

16. See fn. 4 of this chapter.

17. "Foreword" to *Sati*, op. cit., p. XI.

18. *Ibid.*, pp. XII-XIII.

19. Shivasahayaji Chaturvedi, *Satidaha* (Allahabad, Chand Karyalaya, 1926), 106-7. This is the Hindi translation of the "Original Bengali Book by Kumudnath Mullick."

20. Alaka Hejib and Katherine K. Young, "Sati, Widowhood and Yoga" in Arvind Sharma, *Sati*, fn. 363.

21. Romila Thapar, *op. cit.*, p. 16.

    Cf. S. Radha Krishnan.

11

Conclusion

The foregoing account shows that burning of widows was common enough among many ancient tribes and primitive religious communities. Indo-Germanic custom ordained that the wife should die with her husband to provide the diceased with what was dear to him during life. Ancient Greek, German, Slav, Chinese and other civilizations also had similar customs and Kings and nobles were put in their graves with their arms, slaves, servants and ministers. The slaughter of a wife or concubine at the obsequies of a deceased husband seems to have been a Scythian custom.

In the ancient Vedic rite of cremation there is no mention of the sacrifice of the living wife in the burning place of the dead man. The mourners offered cakes and water in the simple belief that the spirits of departed heroes were conscious of such pious attentions, and to this day such a faith lingers in the affections to soften and humanize the world. The *Atharvaveda,* however, refers to a very ancient custom of widow burning which was given up by the Aryans.

The practice is first referred to by Greek historians at the time of Alexander's invasion. The earliest scriptural sanction comes from the *Vishnudharmasutra* written in the early centuries of the Christian era. The first epigraphic record comes from the Gupta period in 510 A.D. The first literary evidence comes from the *Mahabharata*. Thus the practice started in India in the 4th Century B.C. Some tribes like Madras, Bahlikas and Kathais might have practised it but it was not a general practice. It gained momentum during the medieval period and continued up to the early decades of the 19th Century when Bentinck outlawed it. It was quite popular in Kashmir, Rajputana, Bengal, Vijayanagar, Sindh, Karnataka and some other parts of India especially in upper caste families. stray cases of widow-burning are reported even now. The latest case was reported from Rajasthan in 1987.

The *Vishnudharmasutra* mentions Sati as one of the options open to a widow. It recognises the widow as an heir to her husband, allows her to remarry also and she could practise asceticism. But Angiras recommends it and considers it a pious duty of a widow.

There are some verses drawn upon in common, which are found in Parashar, *Brahmapurana* and quoted in the *Mitakshra* commentary on Yajnavalkya and by Apararka and the *Suddhitattva.* According to these verses a Sati dwells in heaven for three and half crores of years. The sati is compared to Arundhati. Harita says that a sati purifies the families of her father, mother and husband.

Padmapurana, Agnipurana, Brhannardiya Purana, Brhaspati, *Suddhitattva,* Apastamba, *Vedavyasa Smriti* and some others recommend it. But there was a difference of opinion as to whether Brahmin widows should perform sati. After sometime Brahmin ladies were permitted to mount the funeral pyre of their husbands. Still it was optional and there were some restrictions also such as women before puberty, with small children, pregnancy and when they are unclean are not to mount the funeral pyre.

In literature we find ample evidence of Sati and they are lauded for their devotion to their husbands. The *Mahabharata, Brahmapurana, Vishnupurana, Kumarsambhava,* Tamil and Kannada literature, *Bhagawatpurana, Mrichchakatika, Kamasutra, Gathasaptasati, Harshacharita, Kadambari, Naishadcharita, Brhtsamhita, Dasakumaracharita,*

Priyadarshika, Nagananda, Sisupalbadha, Rajatarangini, Venisambbara, Kathasaritsagara and many other books refer to sati and eulogise their virtues. Only *Kadambari* protests against this practice.

Kabir has praised the sati for her devotion and love. Amir Khusroe, Muhammad Riza Naui, Shah Abdul Latif, Bharat Chandra, Rama Prasad, Rabindra Nath Tagore and other poets praised the Sati. Thus Sanskrit, Kannada, Tamil, Hindi, Sindhi and Bengali literatures have ample reference to Sati.

We have a large number of inscriptions from Rajputana, Nepal, Karnataka and Maharashtra to show that the practice was prevalent in many parts of India.

Foreign travellers like Alberuni, Ibn Batuta, Friar Jordanus, Sulaiman, Duarte Barbosa, Fernao Nuniz, Nicolo-de-conti, Manucci, Bermier, Tavernier, Thomas Herbert, Petro della valle, Abbe J.A., Dubois, Ralph Fitch, Edwin Arnold, Nicholas Wethington, Todd and a host of Christian missionaries have left their accounts of Sati. They have condemned this inhuman practice but some of them have praised the conjugal fidelity and love and sacrifice for a cause of Indian satis. Some of them have tried to conjecture the reasons for this practice.

Originally the practice was voluntary and optional. The primitive practice was given a colour of wifely devotion and love. It was praised sky-high and Rajput ladies practised it. Later Brahmins also adopted this practice. Still later Sudras and Vaisyas, aspiring for higher social status adopted it. An element of coercion was introduced when widows were drugged and emotionally blackmailed to perform satis . Still later they were forced to commit sati so that their property might be enjoyed by their relations. This was specially the case in Bengal in 18th and early 19th Centuries.

Indian opinion was not unanimous in its favour. Virata, Medhatithi, Vana, Tantra texts condemned this practice as sin and suicide. Social reformers like Sikhguru Amar Das,

Chaitanya, Sankaracharya of Shringeri, Swami Narayan, Rammohan Roy, Mritunjay Vidyalankar and others lent a poweful voice against thia practice. Some journals in early 19th Century supported its abolition. William Bentinck ultimately abolished it in 1829, but sultans of Delhi and Mughal emperors had tried to regulate it. Special permission was required during the Mughal period and a distinction between legal and illegal satis was made.

Even after the abolition of the practice by Bentinck stray cases of sati are reported, the latest being the sati of Roop Kunwar in 1987.

Even after the legal prohibition of this practice, some eminent Indians and even a few foreigners praise the love, fidelity, sense of sacrifice of Indian satis. Thus, Ananda Kentish Coomaraswamy in his "Sati: a Vindication of the Hindu Woman", a paper read before the Sociological Society in London on November 12, 1912 provided a philosophical justification of the rite.[1] With examples of Hindu women burning themselves happily with their dead husbands, Coomarswamy talked about the high ideals of Eastern women which he thought were quite different ideals, were not required to go through a similar process.

Coomaraswamy again took up this theme in his essay on Indian Sati included in his *The Dance of Shiva*.[2] To understand her better he goes to the root of the word which means "essential being". But she who refuses to live when her husband is dead is called Sati in a more special sense, and it is only so that the word (Suttee) is well known to Europeans. "This last proof of the perfect unity of body and soul, this devotion beyond the grave, has been chosen by many Western crities as our reproach, we differ from them in thinking of our 'suttees' not with pity, but with understanding, respect and love. So far from being ashamed of our 'suttees', we take a pride in them; that is even true of the most 'progressive'amongst us".[3]

Coomaraswamy compares the Sati with a patriot who sacrifices his life for a cause—honour of the country. He says that the criticism we make on the institution of Sati and woman's blind devotion is similar to the final judgment we are about to pass on patriotism. We do not, as pragmatists may, resent the denial of the ego for the sake of an absolute, or attach an undue importance to mere life; on the contrary we see clearly that "the reckless and useless sacrifice of the 'suttee' and the patriot is spiritually significant. And what remains perpetually clear is the superiority of the reckless sacrifice to the calculating asertion of right. Criticism of the position of the Indian woman from the ground of assertive feminism, therefore, leaves us entirely unmoved; percisely as the patriot must be unmoved by an appeal to self-interest or a merely utilitarian demonstration of futility. We do not object to dying for an idea as 'suttees' and patriots have died; but we see that there may be other and greater ideas we can better serve by living for them".[4]

He does not accept the allegations that sati must have been a man-made institution imposed on women by men for reasons of their own, or that it was associated with feminine servility, or that it was peculiar to India. According to him, these views are historically unsound. He, however, concedes that in aristocratic circles Sati became to some degree a social convention and pressure was put on unwilling individuals. But again he compares the patriot with the sati and says that just as conscripts are even now forced to suffer or die for other people's ideas, some women might have been forced to commit Sati.

He cites several cases of Sati from Indian literature. One of them is as follows: "In the early Tamil lyrics we read of an earthly bride whom the Brahmans seek to dissuade from the sacrifice; but she answers that since her lord is dead, the cool waters of the lotus pool and the flames of the funeral pyre are alike to her.Another pleads to share her hero's grave, telling the potter that she had fare her lord over many a desert plain, and asking him to make the funeral urn large enough for both".[5]

Coomaraswamy adds that "a man of such towering

genius and spirituality as Kabir so takes for granted the authenticity of the impulse to Sati that he constantly uses it as an image of surrender of the ego to God; and indeed in all Indian mystical literature the love relation of woman to man is taken unhesitatingly as an immediate reflection of spiritual experience. This is most conspicuous in all the Radha-Krishna literature".[6]

P.V. Kane[7] concludes his discussion of Sati in the following words:

> "Modern India does not justify the practice of *Sati*, but it is a warped mentality that rebukes modern Indians for expressing admiration and reverence for the cool and unfaltering courage of Indian women in becoming *Satis* or performing the Jauhar for cherishing their ideals of womanly conduct. If Englishmen can feel pride in their ancestors who grabbed one-fourth of the world's surface or if Frenchmen can feel pride in the deeds of their Emperor Napoleon who tried to enslave the whole of Europe and yet are not held up to ridicule or rebuke, there is no reason why poor Indians cannot express admiration for the sacrifices which their women made in the past, though they may condemn the institution itself which demanded such terrible sacrifice and suffering".

More recently in the controversy in the wake of latest incident of Sati at Deorala in 1987, there have appeared some articles which in a way justify the practice.

Thus, Patrick D. Harrigan, a teacher in the Department of South and South-East Asian Studies at the university of California, wrote an article in November, 1987.[8] In this piece, he describes Roop Kanwar's immolation as voluntary, courageous, "reminiscent of Rajasthan's days of glory". He is upset that it is opposed by "irate" feminists, politicians, and the court so forcing the local police to arrest people and to prevent recurrence.

What astonishes, what "shocks and disappoints" him, is not the immolation for that is the action of a true Rajputni, nor the attempt on the part of a "handful" of English-educated exponents of 'social progress', who are trying to uplift the 'ignorant masses' but rather the "unanimous barrage of rabidly anti-sati sentiment filling the English-language press" and the absence of democratic debate on the "two sides". Fortunately these are not only in the minority, they are also "outsiders", the masses of India approve, respect and admire such acts of courage which are anathema to a "modern mentality".

He does not think the few cases of involuntary sati that are rumoured to have taken place are praiseworthy but even in those the crime is "mitigated by considerations of belief and customs." There is, however, something very wrong with Indian statutory law which "appears to be deadset against Sati in principle". There is something outright criminal about the Indian elite which espouse foreign values with a sense of self-righteousness that is seldom found among foreigners themselves. They propagate these newly acquired values through education, and claim them as superior, resulting in a tyranny of the elect" and an unquestioning acceptance of "anti-traditional" values in the name of modernity and progress. For Harrigan "the modern urban mentality" is the source of all social disease in India e.g., bride burning is far worse than "the traditional rite of self-immolation that is an option for devout and heroic bereaved widows". Sati is "a matter of principle" something we "material pragmatists" cannot comprehend or believe.

He concludes his essay by asserting that "Bharat Mata is great, precisely because her children are free to live and die according to principles. This freedom is in danger of extinction in the face of powerful and ruthlessly intolerant forces masquerading behind an array of good intentions. The time comes for everybody to be brought to account".

Banwari's piece[9] in defence of Hindu culture, attempts to make a moral argument in favour of the heroic and ascetic death. He seems to justify and wants social acceptance of "voluntary" Sati. He makes a case for the subordination of both men and women in their separate domains, to claim that there is no such thing as perfect freedom, and to claim a Buddha that in any case there is no escape from universal unhappiness. *Dharma* is like the conjugal relation, one accepts an imperfect *dharma* precisely as one learns to 'adjust' to an imperfect spouse in marriage. In neither is there any question of divorce.

Secondly, Hinduism is absolutely androgynous—witness shakti, designated as female, the virtues and adjectives used to qualify the gods, the eternal element which is neither male nor female, Shiva as *ardhanarishwar,* and the soul which is born alternately as male and female. Not only did Hinduism achieve all these things without feminist battle but for Banwari 'androgynous' Hinduism seems to be synonymous with social equality between men and women. Further this metaphysical androgyny can compensate for those aspects of Hinduism in which women are regarded as inferior. He tries to prove that Hinduism is not patriarchal and provides equal access to salvation without discriminating between men and women. Spiritually, we are all equals and equally entitled to go to heaven.

Banwari introduces a gender based division of spiritual labour in which living and dying voluntarily through *Sanyas, Kshatra dharma* and *samadhi* are for men while *satidharma* is for women alone. It seems strong social controls are needed to combat the decay of shakti and morality: all kinds of voluntary dying reduce the fear of death in others and build the moral and muscles of a society which can now see the universe as an indivisible consciousness. It would be barbaric and unfair to expect bravery and sacrifice from men alone who follow *Kshatradharma* on the battlefield. The implication here is that if only men are warriors, then in the interest of gender equality we should accept that only women will be satis. Bravery (and by implication Sati) is a momentary impulse to risk life but this very impulse is a gift of our *sanskaras* which uphold sacrifice for a high ideal as real courage. A sati is a woman firm on *sati, sat* derives from *satya* and means total faith and belief in the husband. Men are expected to have many kinds of devotion for truth but they are not expected to have devotion for *sat*, for this *satitva* we have to look to women such as Savitri and Anasuya.

Banwari tries to separate *satitva* as a concept and then claims that women do not immolate themselves for love of their husbands but rather the husband is a medium, a Vehicle for their own salvation. A woman would want to immolate herself with her husband not for love of the physical man but for her own *satyanishtha*, he is the vehicle for her own devotion, self-control, belief in Truth, and such an act is one of courage not cowardice.

He proceeds to make a case for the exceptional sati; since he is determined to retain the concept of *satitva* he is ready to denounce the practice to sati—to some extent. First he claims all the above is a principled definition and does not apply to ordinary satis where the women decide because of custom, family prestige. Psychological pressure and obscurantism. To be a Sati a woman needs courage, inner strength and other such qualities which are acquired through great preparation. Without all this Sati is merely an unauthorised, unrightful act of forced martyrdom and should be discouraged because it cheapens the concept.

He feels that as a common custom it was legitimate under Muslim and British rule but would be excessive now. The symbolic value accrued from an occasional sati is sufficient for us to maintain our *sanskaras*. "The social order should make it nearly impossible for any woman to become Sati. "However, we must not denounce *sat* and *satitva* for such denunciation will ruin our self confidence and narrow our very souls. All we need is the exceptional Sati.

Banwari sticks throughout to the idea that it is women who decide to immolate themselves. By asserting that Roop Kanwar's sati was voluntary, he accuses the westernized modernists who have claimed that Roop was forced into the pyre, of destroying the glory of women and the sanctity of tradition, of rallying in support of a state and a legal machinery which has no credibility and is ineffectual anyway. Finally neither the State nor the Westernized modernists care about the ordinary people.

Banwari ends in a mood of confrontative optimism: "the ordinary people of the country are getting extremely agitated about their beliefs and are ready to confront the entire structure of the State, not only must we all take sides and choose between the people and the westernized elite, but from such a confrontation itself, the strength to face the challenge of western culture may arise".[10]

Ashis Nandy in his essay "The Sociology of Sati"[11] criticises the modernists for their inconsistency. If Sati is to be condemned, so is the suicide by Jaina *munis* or death of young-men killed in wars. Hence modernists should condemn all forms of suicide to show their consistency.

Moreover, westernized modernists are alienated from the rural masses who appear to them as 'self-destructive', 'superstitions' and 'invite censure', thus providing the complacent modernist urbanites with both a spectacle and a claim to moral superiority.

Nandy considers sati as the 'pathology of colonialism not of Hinduism', but he concedes it has 'something to do with tradition'. This pathology only emerges 'when the traditional way of life began to collapse due to the onslaught of outside forces'. If undisturbed and left to themselves, Hindu traditions would be satisfied with a few incidents and would not need to resort to epidemics of widow immolation as when Vijayanagar Kingdom was collapsing or when Rajput principalities were under attack or when Britain was consolidating its power in India.

This succinct history of Sati, however, does not touch upon the real issues. It may be that Lord Bentinck's prohibition of Sati by law did not stop the practice completely. Recent flurry in Rajasthan exposes another side of the problem. The religious merit of a woman committing sati is nowadays translated in terms of fabulous material gain for the family of the deceased. Some times millions of rupees are raised in donation for erecting a sati temple, which gives substantial annual family income for generations to come. So the allure of sati is sometimes too much to be ignored.

What is the real issue? Sati can claim to have legitimacy only when it truly amounts to a case of active religious suicide; "active" because it must be distinguished from the passive acceptance of death by martyrs. Sati is not martyrdom. To describe Sati as "widow-burning" is already a falsification. Besides, most outsiders think of sati as something virtually forced upon the individual by the norms of Hindu society. This is wrong. The norms of the society never demanded it. And active religious suicide must be distinguished from the forced ending of one's life. It is true that the position of a widow in Hindu society generally was and has been so precarious and painful that suicide would be preferable. But if one is inspired to end one's life for this reason, it can hardly be called sati, for religious motivation would be lacking. Hence, I find it hard to agree with some feminists today who claim that Sati is only symptomatic of the extent of torture of women in Hindu society. The torture of women has been present almost to the same extent (sometimes even more) in many Asian societies, but there has been no Sati or widow burning there.

Nobody can dispute the fact that in a majority of the cases of reported sati, there was inducement, brain washing, allurement of a happy after-life, etc. Sometimes physical force and drugs have been used. All these cases would by the same token be disqualified from being cases of Sati, of active religious suicide.

There are only two types of suicide closest to sati:

> (1) martyrdom for the cause of one's religion; (2) *sallekhana,* suicide of Jain monks. If sati has any rational Justification, it must be shared by the other two. A pertinent question is, of course, why and how can one justify Christian martyrdom but condemn

sati unequivocally? A simple answer is: most Christians who condemn sati invariably look upon it not as an active religious suicide but as a barbaric practice of "widow-burning" by the heathens".

But even if we ignore such prejudices or misrepresentations, or what could presumably be called the colonial rulers reading of the Indian situation, we must face the following question: can one support without prejudice the Christian martyrdom as well as the Jain monks *sallekhana* suicide and at the same time condemn sati? If religion is regarded as the "opiate" of the people, then of course the three would be in the same boat. But if religion is something more than that, then the answer to it is yes, we can. Let me explain briefly.

The three types of suicide noted here would fall under the category that E. Durkheim called "altruistic", or even "acute altruistic suicide". In a way, any suicide is a form of egoism But still religious martyrs die for keeping a faith alive and death is usually forced upon them by circumstances (there were 400 martyrs during the reign of Bloody Mary). Their choice is thus limited, for the alternative is even more demeaning. However, Sati is by definition voluntary in Hinduism.

A Jain monk must first live long enough to be old and must devote his entire life to his *sadhana* to achieve *nirvana* and it is only at the end, in order not to be a burden to others, that he decides to quietly end his life by retiring to a forest and not making any effort to procure food. Under such ideal conditions, this seems to be the least violent way of ending one's life, and if there is egoism, it is least reprehensible, here morally, sati, by contrast, is usually the case of a young woman, and her resolution to end her life has every chance of being the result of a temporary depression which would certainly pass away with time. Moreover, Sati is often described as a short-cut passport to heaven by the texts that approve it. These texts even say that an unchaste wife should perform sati to have a clear entry to heaven:

> Sati is after all suicide exhibiting an extreme form of violence and cruelty. We do not know how many genuine Sati cases there have been in history, where genuineness consists in their being on par with the Jain monks in terms of their lifelong commitment to religiosity. There may have been some. But despite the proliferation of sati temples, it is wrong to put the majority of modern satis on a high pedestal along with the Jain or Hindu monks, For surely, even the resolution for suicide at the death of her husband may simply be, even if not induced by anybody, frustrating sense of maladjustment to the new situation where life may seem to be losing its meaning—a case that Durkheim rightly called "anomic" suicide. And this type of suicide can not be allowed, both legally and morally.[12]

One hundred and sixty four years after it was banned, we find ourselves in the peculiar position of having to justify and defend our stand against the practice of sati. We have to restate the case against barbarism, exhume legal and other arguments long laid to rest; reiterate the imperative of a truly secular state and its consequent, social responsibilities and try valiantly to keep the wolves of Church and state from howling at our doors.

The sanctity of tradition and the freedom to practise one's religion cannot and should not allow the murder of widows. If scriptural pronouncements (though these are doubtful in the case of sati) are to regulate our moral and judicial conduct, a case for polygamy, untouchability, child marriage, etc. can also be made. Where do we go then?

REFERENCES

1. "Sati: A Defense of the Indian Women," *The Sociological Review,* April, 1913.
2. Ananda Coomaraswamy, *The Dance of Shiva* (New Delhi: Sagar Publications, 1971), pp. 111ff.

3. *Ibid.*, pp. 111-12.
4. *Ibid.*, p. 112.
5. *Ibid.*, p. 113.
6. *Ibid.*
7. P.V. Kane, *History of Dharmasastra,* Vol. II, Part-I (Poona: Bhandarkar Oriental Research Institute, 1941), p. 636.
8. Patrick D. Harrigan, "Tyranny of the Elect? Bringing Bharat Mata up to Date," *The Statesman*, Delhi, dt. 5.11.1987.
9. Banwari, "Nar-Nari Sambandh," *Jansatta* dt. 29.9.87 to 1.10.87 For a very good summary of this article with comments, see Kumkum Sangari, "Persesuating the Myth," *Seminar*, February, 1988, pp. 28-29.
10. Kumkum Sangari, *op. cit.*, p. 29.
11. Ashish Nandi "The Sociology of Sati," *The Indian Express*, dt. 5.10.1987.
12. B.K. Motilal, "Sati: An outrage or a shortcut to Heaven," *The Times of India*, subsequicentennial issue, Nov.-Dec., 1988.

Bibliography

(a) Books

Agnipurana.

Atharva Veda.

Apasthamba, *Grihyasutra.*

Brahmapurana.

Bharat Chandra Granthavli, Basumati Edn.

Bhagavatapurana.

Bhasa, *Urubhanga.*

Bhasa, *Dutaghatotkacha.*

Bana, *Harshacharita.*

Bana, *Kadambari.*

Dandi, *Dasakumaracharitam.*

Epigraphia Carnatica, Vol. VIII.

Hala, *Gathasaptasati.*

Herodotus, IV, V.

Harsha - *Priyadashika.*

Harsha - *Nagananda.*

Kumarsambhava.

Kalidas, *Abhigyan Sakuntalam.*

Mahanirvana Tantra.

Magha - *Sisupalabadha.*

Mahabharata.

Parashar Madhaviya.

Padmapurana.

Rgveda.

Ramayana.

Ram Prasad Granthavali, Basumati Edn.

Suddhitatwa.

Sudraka, *Mrichakatika.*

Taittiriya Aranyaka.

Vedvyas Smriti.

Vishnupurana.

Visnumriti.

Vedic Index, vol. I.

Vayu Purana.

Vatsyayana, Kamsutra, Vol. VI.

Varahmihira, *Brihatsamhita.*

Venisamhara.

Vrisotsargavidhi (Ms Durbar Library, Kathmandu).

A.A. Macdonell, *The Vedic Mythology* (Varanasi : Indological Book House, 1971).

A.A. Macdonell, *A History of Sanskrit Literature* (London: William Heinemann, 1913).

A.S. Altekar, *The Position of Women in Hindu Civilisation* (Delhi: Motilal Banarasidas, 1962).

Abbe J.A. Dubois, *Hindu Manners, Customs and Ceremonies* (Oxford: Clarendon press, 1953).

A.C. Banerjee, *The State and Society in Northern India* (1206-1526) (Calcutta: K.P. Bagchi & Co., 1982).

Allchin, Bridget and Raymond, *The Birth of Indian Civilization*, 1968.

Ananda K. Coomaraswamy, "Sati: A Defence of the Indian Woman," *The Sociological Review*, London, 1913.

Anand K. Coomaraswamy, *The Dance of Shiva* (New Delhi: Sagar Publications, 1971).

Arvind Sharma, Sati (Delhi: Motilal Banarasidas, 1988).

Azir Ahmad, *Studies in Islamic Culture in the Indian Environment* (Oxford: Clarendon Press, 1964).

Bhagawat Sharam Upadhyaya, *Women in Rgveda* (Benaras: Nandkishore and Bros., 1941).

Calcutta Journal, 1820.

Charles Rockwell Lanman, *A Sanskrit Reader* (Harvard H.V.P. 1971).

Crooke, *Popular Religion and Folklore of Northern India.*

Christoph Von Furer-Haimendorf, *The Aboriginal Tribes of Hyderabad*, Vol. III.

D.A. Girrbing (ed.), *Everyman's Encyclopaedia*, Vol. XI (London: J.M. Dent & Sons Ltd., 1978).

D.C. Sen, *Brhata Banga*, VOl. II.

D.C. Sircar, *Select Inscriptions*, VOl. I.

D.D. Kosambi, *Myth and Reality* (Bombay: Popular Prakashan, 1962).

D.D. Kosambi, *The Culture and Civilization of Ancient India in Historical Outline* (Delhi: Vikas, 1975).

Demetrius Charles de Kavanagh Boulger, *Lord William Bentinck* (Oxford: Clarendon Press, 1892).

D.K.R. Patil, *Cultural History from the Vayu Purana.*

Encyclopaedia Americana, Vol. XXVI (New York: Americana Corporation, 1974).

Edward Thompson, *Suttee* (London: George Allen and Unwin, 1928). *Epigraphia Carnatica*, Vols. IV & VIII.

E.I. Vols. VI, XIV, XX, X, XVI.

Elliot and Dowson, *History of India Told by its own Historians*, Vol. I, (London, 1866).

Epigraphia Carnatica, Vol. IV.

Fleet, *C.I.I.*, Vol. III.

H.H. Wilson, *Works*, Vol. II.

G.B. Malleson, *Emperor Akbar* (New Delhi: Asian Publication Services, 1978).

H.T. Sorely, *Shah Abdul Latif of Bhit* (Oxford: OUP, 1940.

Hiralal, *Inscriptions from C.P.*

H.T. Colebrooke, *Miscellaneous Essays*, Vol. I.

H.T. Colebrooke, "On the Duties of a faithful Widow," *The Asiatic Researches*, Vol. IV, Calcutta, 1795.

Harendra Nath Maitra, *Hinduism: The World Ideal* (New York: Dodd, Mead & Co., 1916).

Indra, *The Status of Women in Ancient India* (Delhi: Motilal Banarasidas, 1955).

Indian Antiquary, Vol. IX, IV.

Ibn Batuta translated and selected by Gible (London: 1929).

Indrajeet Kaur, *Status of Hindu Women in India* (Allahabad: Chugh, 1983).

James Hustings (ed.) *Encyclopaedia of Religion and Ethics*, Vol. XI (Edinberg T. & Clark, 1958).

J. Talboys Wheeler, *India from the Earliest Ages* (Delhi: Cosmo Publications, 1973).

J.Talboys Wheeler, *India of the Vedic Age* (Delhi: Cosmo Publications, 1973).

James Talboys Wheeler, *Ancient and Hindu India: The Brahmani Period* (Calcutta: Punthi Pustak, 1961).

Journal of Asiatic Society of Bengal, 1935.

J.B. Tavernier, *Travels in India* (Oxford: 1925).

John Daswon (ed.) *Akbarnama* (Calcutta: Susil Gupta (India) Pvt. Ltd., 1959.

John. Malcolm (Tr.), *Tuzuk-i-Jahangiri,* Vol. II.

J. Brandel, *The Wheels of COmmerce* (New York, 1979).

Kalhana *Rajatarangini* (Tr. M.A. Stein), Delhi: Motilal Banarasidas, 1961).

Kenneth Ingham, *Reformers in India,* 1793-1833 (Cambridge: U.P., 1956).

Keralacharam (Calicut: Collectorate Press, 1866).

Kumudnath Mullick, *Satidaha* (Tr. Shiva Sahayji Chaturvedi, (Allahabad: Chand Karyalaya, 1926).

Majumdar & Altekar, *The Vakataka Gupta Age* (Delhi: Motilal Banarasidas, 1967).

Macanliffe, *The Sikh Religion,* Vol. II, (Oxford, 1909).

M. Mujeeb, *The Indian Muslims* (London: George Allen & Unwin Ltd. 1967).

Monier Williams, *Indian Wisdom* (London: H. Allen & Co., 1875).

M.H. Ramasharma, *The History of the Vijayanagar Empire,* Vol. I (Bombay: Popular Prakashan, 1978).

M.L. Bhagi, *Ancient India—Culture and Thought* (Ambala Cant, N.D.)

N.M. Penzer (ed.), *The Ocean of Story,* Vol. IV (London: Chas. J. Sawyer, 1925).

Nayan Tara Sahgal, *Prison and Chocolate.*

P.V. Kane, *History of Dharmasastra,* Vol. II, Part I (Poona: Bhandarkar Oriental Research Institute, 1941).

P. Thomas, *Indian WOmen Through the Ages* (London: Asia, 1964).

Philip, Woodruff, *The Men who Ruled India,* Vol. I, (London: Jonathan Cape, 1953).

P.N. Ojha, *Glimpses of Social Life in Mughal India* (New Delhi: Classical Publications, 1979).

R.C. Majumdar (ed.) *THe Age of Imperial Unity* (Bombay: Bhartiya Vidyabhavan, 1953).

Report on the Archaeological Survey of India, Vols. VIII, VII, X, IX.

Romila Thapar, *"In History,"* Seminar, New Delhi, Feb. 1988.

R. Sewell, *A Forgotten Empire* (London: Swan Connenschhein, 1900).

R.C. Iachner, *Hinduism* (Oxford: Clarendon Press, 1962).

Ramchandra Prasad, *Early English Travellers in India* (Delhi: Motilal Banarasidas, 1965).

Raymond Brady Williams, *A New face of Hinduism: The Swamivarayan Religion* (Cambridge: CUP, 1984).

Ram Mohan Roy, *The Practice of Burning Widows Alive* 9Calcutta, 1818).

Ram Mohan Roy, Translation of a Conference between on Advocate and an opponent of the Practice of Burning Widows Alive from Original Bungla (Calcutta: Ram Mohan Roy, 1818).

Reginald Heber, *Narrative of a Journey Through the Upper Provinces of India* (London, 1961).

R.H. Aitken, *Suttee* (Bombay: N.p., 1872).

R.R. Diwakar (ed.) *Bihar Through The Ages.*

A.I.R., 1913.

Strabo, *India,* Sect. 30.

Seminar, New Delhi: Feb. 1988.

South Indian Epigraphical Reports, 1907.

S. Setter and G.D. Sontheimer, *Memorial Stores* (Dharwad, 1982).

Sudesh Vaid, *"Politics of Widow Immolation,"* Seminar, Feb. 88.

"Sati in Hyderabad," Proceedings of Indian History Congress, 1953.

Strabo Hamilton and Falconer's translation, Vol. IV.

Sachan, *Alberuni's India* (London: 1914), Vol. I.

Sushil Choudhary, *"A Note on Sati in Medieval India,"* Proceedings of Indian History Congress, 1964.

S. Pearce Carey, *William Carey* (London, 1924).

Sukla Das, *Socio-Economic Life of Northern India* (New Delhi: Abhinar Publications, 1980).

Schrader, Pre-historic Antiquities of the ryan Peoples (London: 1890).

Tawney, *Kathasaritsagara,* Vol. IV, (Bombay: 1903).

The Travels of Peter Mundy, 1914.

Todd, *Annals,* Vols. I, II.

The National Herald, Lucknow.

The Statesman, Calcutta.

Amar Ujala, Agra.

The Search Light, Patna.

The Times of India, Delhi.

Upendra Nath Ball, *Ram Mohan Roy* (Calcutta: U Roy & Sons, 1933).

Upendra Thakur, *The History of Suicide in India* (Delhi: Munshiram Manoharlal, 1963).

V.N. Dutta, *Sati* (New Delhi: Manohar Books, 1988).

Vijnaneswara, *Mitakshra.*

V.S. Agrawal "Terracotta Figurines of Ahicchatra, District Barelly, U.P." in *Ancient India,* No. 4.

Vijaya Lakshmi Pandit, *The Scope of Happiness: A Personal Memoir* (London: Weidenfeld and Nicolson, 1979).

William Crooke (ed.), *Sir H.Yule and A.C. Burnell's Hobson-Jobson* (Delhi: Munshiram Manoharlal, 1968).

Westermarck, *Origin and Development of Moral Ideas,* Vol. I, 1906.

W.M. Thinders Petrie, *Religious Life in Ancient Greek.*

William Dwight Whitney, *Atharvaveda-Samhita,* Vol. II (Delhi: Motilal Banarasidas, 1971).

Walsh, "Verakal and Sati-Memorial Stores at Budhpur and Buram," *Journal of Bihar and Orissa Research Society,* Vol. XXIII.

William Johns, *A Collection of facts and opinions Relative to the Burning of Widows with the Dead Bodies of their Husbands* (Birmingham W.H. Pearce, 1816).

(b) Articles

Ashis Nandy, "Sociology of Sati", *Indian Express,* 5 Oct. 87.

B.K. Chattopadhyay, "Sati," *Statesman,* 5 March 72.

Barun Dasgupta, "Sati controversy in Calcutta," *Mainstream,* 19 Dec. 87.

Brinda Karat, "Deorala: Socio-economic roots of Women's subjugation," *Hindustan Times,* 9 Oct. 87.

Girish M. Vakil, "Myth of Voluntary Sati", *Eve's Weekly,* 7 Feb. 81.

Iqbal Kaul, "Husband's rights, Wife's Rites," *Times of India,* 3 Jan. 88.

Iqbal Kaul, "The Origin of Sati," *Illustrated Weekly of India,* 18 Jan. 81.

Jeevan Kulkarni, "Sati: Shame or Pride," *Organiser,* 22 Nov. 87.

Kumkum Sangri, "Perpetuating the Myth," *Seminar,* Feb. 88.

M.V. Kamath, "Sati: The SHame of a nation," *Illustrated Weekly of India,* 15 April 1980.

Milap Chand Dandia, "Celebration of a death," *Telegraph,* 6 Oct. 1987.

N. Vishwanath, "When all the World was a pyre," *Times of India,* 28 Feb. 84.

Nandita Brahma, "Sati," *Statesman,* 23 March 72.

Nikhil Chakravartty, "Why is the Congress reluctant to condemn Sati?," *Telegraph*, 27 Sept. 87.

Poonam Dadas, "Gender Theme—Sati raises its ugly head," *Amrit Bazar Patrika*, 19 Sept. 87.

Ragni Bakshi, "The Rajput revival," *Illustrated Weekly of India*, Oct. 87.

Rajendra Prasad Jain, "How they look at Sati?" *Organiser*, 15 No. 87.

Romila Thapar, "In History," *Seminar*, Feb. 88.

Romila Thapar, "Through the ages," *Seminar*, Dec. 63.

S.K. Ahuja, "The Legend that was Sati," *Folklore*, March 1970.

Sudesh Vaid, "Politics of WIdow Immolation," Seminar, Feb. 88.

Sudhanshu Mishra, "Sati: fortune behind the crime," *Link* 27 Sept. 87.

Surendra Mohan, "Pernicious Practice of Sati," *Janata*, 18 Oct. 87.

Tara Ali Baig, "Who says the sati system is dead?" *Femina*, Dec. 83.

Vasudha Dhagamwar, "Saint Vichim or Criminal," *Seminar*, Feb. 88.

Vimal Balasubrahmanyam, "No girls please, we are Indians," *Mainstream*, March 86.

Zarina Ahmed, "A Case Study," *Seminar*, Dec. 1964.

Index

■■■